PICK GUNS

Lock Picking for Spies, Cops, and Locksmiths

John Minnery

PALADIN PRESS
BOULDER, COLORADO

Pick Guns: Lock Picking for Spies, Cops, and Locksmiths
by John Minnery

Copyright © 1989 by John Minnery

ISBN 0-87364-510-3
Printed in the United States of America

Published by Paladin Press, a division of
Paladin Enterprises, Inc., P.O. Box 1307,
Boulder, Colorado 80306, USA.
(303) 443-7250

Direct inquiries and/or orders to the above address.

Contents

Dedication

"L.C.'s"

Acknowledgments

The author wishes to express his gratitude to the following individuals who made this book possible:

H. Keith Melton, Curator, Clandestine Services Museum (private), who was unstinting with his aid on lock-picking devices.

Morris Moses of Albany, New York, who provided the author with his initial research on this subject.

Khristine Balingit of Toronto, Canada, once my apprentice and an extraordinary lock picker in her own right, who developed the metered tension wrench and was of great assistance in researching patents for me.

Fellow locksmiths and apprentices. In Canada: Bob Salembier of Simcoe, Ontario; David Sloot of Brantford, Ontario; and Carole McGrath of Brantford, Ontario. In the United States: Terukazu Miyamoto and Mr. Carter of Ford Locksmiths, Detroit, Michigan; Mr. Dan Dwyer (retired) of Kelly's Locksmithing, Boston, Massachusetts.

The staff of Art-Ex, Brantford, Ontario.

Your encouragement and support were sincerely appreciated.

Introduction

Locks are, in a real sense, sacred. They protect our valuables and even our very lives. To be entrusted with the keys to a lock has always been held to be a great honor. On the other hand, to have a lock not open or to lose keys are considered reasons to feel ashamed.

The ability to open locks without keys is thought to be iconoclastic magic. It is one of the few remaining awe-inspiring events in a world where mechanical marvels and electronic wonders are boringly commonplace.

The secrets of lock picking have always been jealously guarded by the locksmithing priesthood. Quite apart from the most obvious reason of public safety, it is also because they themselves only dimly understand what they do and how they do it.

The lock picking gun took the art of lock picking out of the Dark Ages and democratized the ability to open locks by mechanical means.

Skill, it is true, is still needed. Some professional locksmiths have never been able to use a gun and still prefer their pick sets. By and large, however, the pick gun has been a boon to the professional and a terrific aid to law enforcement and even national security.

Criminals, alas, also use pick guns, as do private detectives, industrial spies, and government agents. In this book we are interested in the pick gun only and not its wielder. *Please do not abuse this knowledge.*

Chapter One

Let's Rap About Locks

The modern pin-tumbler lock can trace its origins back to the Temple of Karnak in ancient Egypt. During those times, locks were made of wood and used on warehouse gates and courtyard portals. When the bolt was slid across to lock the gate, wooden peg tumblers fell (or tumbled) into recesses in the bolt, thereby preventing it from being drawn back to open the gate again. This arrangement relied on gravity to keep the pegs in their blocking positions between the upper and lower chambers. In order to withdraw the bolt, it was necessary to lift the pegs back up to their previous upper-chamber positions within the lock housing. To do this, a key was required.

The key was introduced into a key slot underneath the bolt. It had projecting pegs that corresponded with the tumbler recesses within the bolt. The key was then lifted upward and held horizontally against the bolt to allow the tumbler pegs to nest once again in their upper chambers and clear the bolt of its obstruction. The bolt was now free to be slid back so the gate could be opened.

This type of lock, in exactly the form described, was used in Egypt until the ousting of the Ottoman Turks—some four thousand years! It is also worth noting that

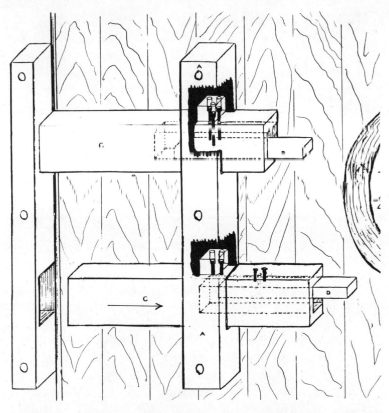

Ancient Egyptian locks. The upper bolt is shown locked with key D inserted. This lock had three pins and the key belonged to the Egyptian master. The lower lock is shown with the bolt withdrawn by means of a two-peg key. It belonged to a trusted slave.

The key to the upper lock worked in both locks, since it could lift all the pins to shear line. The key was introduced into the locks through a hole in the door.

The arrangement of pins and pegs was arbitrary and varied widely.

similar locks were used in the Faeroe Islands (just north of the Shetlands) until modern times. It is possible that the inhabitants, descendants of Norse Vikings, were introduced to these locks when their ancestors brought them back from trading with (or perhaps raiding) Egyptians during the Dark Ages.

Modern pin-tumbler locks were invented by Linus Yale, Sr., and were incorporated in his Yale Bank Locks made at his factory in Newport, New York. These locks, however, were only the pronounen of the pin-tumbler cylinder, designed by his son, Linus Yale, Jr.

Linus Yale, Jr., was born in Salisbury, New York, in 1821. In his youthful ambition, he wanted to be an artist, but he had inherited his father's mechanical genius and went to work with him designing bank locks. The junior Yale used his talents to develop better and more intricate locks of the bank and treasury type. He finally did away with the lock's weak spot, the key, when he introduced the first modern dial-combination lock.

Linus Yale, Sr. (left), and Linus Yale, Jr.

Concurrent to Yale's lock work, there was a tremendous upheaval in the lock world. A.C. Hobbs, a brash and talented American, had tweaked British craftsmanship and pride by picking the best of the British bank locks. This momentous event took place in 1851, while a grand exhibition of British industry was being held, and it caused world attention to shift to America for the design and production of better locks.

Linus Yale's final efforts (he died in 1868) were directed toward perfecting the pin-tumbler locks his father had worked with and making them available to the public at large. As a result, Yale's name became synonymous with locks in general and locks of excellent quality in particular. The company grew and prospered under the direction of Henry Towne, with whom Yale had formed a partnership the summer before he died. Yale truly made the world a more secure place in which to live.

* * * * * * *

Pin-tumbler locks of today are made by many different lock companies from all over the world. Their quality runs the gamut from excellent to shoddy. If you want to learn about picking locks—and pick guns in particular—you will have to learn to dismantle pin-tumbler locks.

The following materials are required:
- (a) One new replacement night latch rim cylinder (low-cost or imported is OK) with key;
- (b) Tweezers (eyebrow or sliver-removal type);
- (c) Screwdriver;
- (d) Pliers;
- (e) Wooden dowel (.5-inch diameter, 4 inches long).

The following materials are not required but helpful:
- (a) .002-inch metal shim (.75-inch wide, 1.5 inches long, curved over the width, .75-inch radius);
- (b) Old sock with toe removed, or plastic bag with bottom sliced open.

There will be a tailpiece projecting from the rear of the rim cylinder. This must be removed either by unscrewing two small retaining screws or by withdrawing a retainer clip.

Have the old sock or plastic bag handy. Put the lock cylinder in the bag and hold on to it, with your left hand holding the cylinder and your right hand the key. Put the key into the *plug*—the inner cylinder with the keyhole (*keyway*). Turn the key slightly and pull . . .

Surprise!

Five springs and five pairs of tumblers will go flying in all directions, especially if you neglected to use the sock or plastic bag. Gather everything up again, as you'll be needing them later.

Arrange the cylinder's entrails in front of you and examine them. Their intricacy might seem intimidating to the beginner, but notice that the pins are different lengths and half of them are pointed at one end. These are the lower pins that fit into the plug that was just pulled out. Put the key back into the plug and drop a pin, point first, into a chamber. It will either ride above the plug, drop below it, or rest even with the plug's surface, in which case it is one of the correct pins for the key's combination of cuts. In this manner you can arrange all the pins so they correspond to the cuts of the key.

The upper pins are flat on both ends and are usually called *drivers* because, under the influence of their springs, they drive the lower pins downward. The location where the upper and lower pins meet within the lock (when the proper key is inserted) is called the *shear line*. It is here where the mating surfaces of the two pins will slide, allowing the plug to turn.

You may notice *chamfering* on the pins, which encourages this mating and turning process. You will observe now and should be aware forever that *tolerance* also plays a major part at this juncture of shearing surfaces. Tolerance is what makes picking possible and, although it is vital to good lock design and construction, too much tolerance—caused during manufacture or by wear—lessens a lock's security by making the possibility of picking probable.

Now take the half-inch wooden dowel—hereafter called the *follower*—and see if it will fit into the plug hole in the cylinder. Some sanding may be necessary to achieve a good fit. Pull the follower sufficiently out of the plug to expose the rearmost upper chamber. Using your tweezers, place a spring into the chamber. Pick up an upper pin with your tweezers and press it into the chamber above the spring. By coordinating your grip on the pin with the pressure being exerted rearward as you push the follower, you will be able to bind the pin so it will be half in and half out of the chamber.

With the follower binding the pin, you will now be able to release the tweezer's grip and use its points to press the exposed base of the pin and force it into the chamber. The follower will override the pin and it will remain nested there.

Take the plug in your hand and put the correct bottom pin in its last chamber. Reintroduce the plug to the front of the cylinder and use it to push the slave-pin follower out the rear. They must move in unison, as any gap will allow the spring-driven upper pin to pop between.

You now have what amounts to a simple pin-tumbler lock using a single set of pins and one spring. Your key will turn the plug and when you withdraw it (be careful here, since there is no retainer), the cylinder will be locked. It is ideal for introductory practice work.

If you push in only the *point* of your key and give it a slight twist, you will find the shear line as the pin rides up the ramp of the key's nose (*tip*). Even if you use a blank key, it would behave in the same fashion. By using a .002-inch shim, it is possible to pass through the juncture of the pins along the shear line to each pin in succession as it is raised to the shear line. Once separated by the shim, the lock will open by *shimming,* a standard locksmithing technique. (For more information on this and other basic locksmithing techniques, refer to any standard reference text on locksmithing.)

The next locksmithing technique is known as *rapping*. Take the cylinder in your hand and invert it with the upper chambers facing down. With your forefinger, gently press the rear of the plug inward. You might feel a slight "give," so don't proo too hard. Grasp the lock solidly with the rest of your fingers and knock it against a bench or tabletop, as you would when cracking a hard-boiled egg. Be careful not to mash your fingertips in the process!

This action, in conjunction with the pressure on the plug, should allow the plug to suddenly move forward when the pins are jostled to the shear line. What is meant to happen here is that the striking force of hitting the lock against the bench is transferred to the pins through the medium of inertia. The impact on the lock acts on the lower pin, which in turn moves the upper pin, and for a brief interval they split, creating a wide, gapping shear line. At that instant, the gentle pressure you have maintained on the plug will take over and it will shift out of the cylinder. If you have pressed too hard at this time, the plug might pop out of the cylinder and you could lose the upper pin and spring.

For those of you who are unsuccessful, you should vary the degree of striking force you apply against the cylinder. Be aware that you are trying for impact transference and it is an acquired skill. It is initially hard to learn but, once learned, it is never forgotten.

The rest of you who were able to do this task with little problem should now load the fourth chamber with its respective pins and spring and try the rapping technique again. This should be continued until all five chambers are loaded. The difficulty increases as the chambers are filled, so you may need lots of practice to master this rapping act. You also may want to rearrange the combination of pins to give some variation and further test your skills.

In the old days, rapping was the accepted practice when

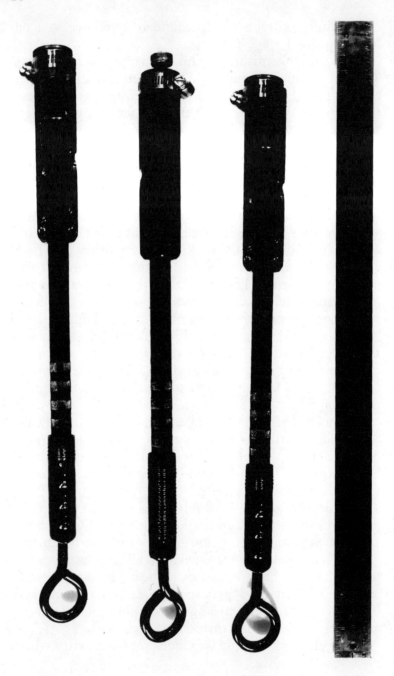

The Raven Rapping Jig (on facing page) designed by the author. A rim or mortise-lock cylinder is secured into the "V" trough of the angle iron by means of a hose clamp. The tailpiece (or *cam*) must first be removed from the rear of the lock. A spring-loaded dowel that acts as a plunger and follower bears on the lock's plug. This is adjustable by means of the threaded eyebolt. A stop has to be located at the front of the cylinder to prevent the plug from moving forward too far when it is successfully rapped open.

The handle of the Raven Rapper is grasped and the lock is struck against a square of carpeting laid on a bench. The lock is rapped upside down in this technique, just as it is during hand rapping.

The above photo shows a rim-cylinder Corbin lock that has been successfully rapped. The plug has been rotated prior to servicing disassembly.

The forward-movement adjusting screw and thumbnut can clearly be seen. This should allow a little less than one-eighth inch of forward movement of the plug when rapped.

Some locks have six chambers, only five of which are generally used. If the plug moves too far forward, there is danger of the pins aligning with the next forward chamber, which will relock the lock. This situation is bad enough, but with a previously empty chamber, the results are catastrophic and the lock becomes difficult to service. This is an unnecessary headache that can be avoided with a little foresight.

locksmiths needed to open cylinders for servicing when no key was available. Hollow depressions would be worn into workbenches where locksmiths habitually rapped their cylinders. Of course, there are other methods of rapping. The lock can be held in your hand and the bottom of the lock cylinder struck with a wooden mallet or even a hammer handle.

Personally, I've found that rapping is a real pain, chiefly in the fingertips, and there is added frustration when the plug shifts too far and the upper pins drop into the adjacent chambers. Then you have to start all over again. If the lock has six chambers and only five are filled, then generally the upper pin has dropped into an empty bottom chamber, with disastrous results. It can be serviced, but it's a real pain, chiefly in the bottom. (To overcome this difficulty, I have designed a rapping jig named after Poe's pet: The Raven.)

* * * * * * *

The now exasperated reader might well ask what all this has to do with a book about lock-pick guns. It is this precise point that I have been leading to: All modern lock-pick guns rely on this impact transfer to pick locks. However, *they rap the pins, instead of the lock.* This was a major step forward in the art of lock picking. At the moment the pick gun was invented, the art became subject to mechanical science and a great deal of mystery went out of lock work.

With pick guns, locks could be picked (rapped) on site, entry gained, and locks serviced by the locksmith or evidence collected by the investigator. This was the profound advance this device fostered, for it no longer was necessary for locksmiths to spend years at their craft in order to successfully pick locks. A rookie detective could learn the technique with a few hours of instruction and practice. The development of the lock-pick gun was, indeed, a quantum leap in the evolution of lock picking.

Chapter Two

The Father of the Pick Gun

We know locks can be rapped open as a service technique, and padlocks and handcuffs can be opened by rapping as well. The goal is to get the locking bolt itself to spring back and release the shackle. Generally speaking, modern padlocks and handcuffs do not respond to this action, but at the turn of the century they could be bounced open with practice and skill.

The great Harry Houdini wore a lead block on a belt hidden under his suit. On occasion, he also wore a sheet of metal around his upper leg. These belts acted as his "benches" to strike his locks against while handcuffed. Houdini also was not above "doctoring" the locks used in his act by substituting weakened springs to make his escape more certain. Indeed, he was well acquainted with locks and locksmithing and did much to publicize locks and security and—perversely—how to thwart them.

It was at this time that the pick gun was born.

The patent drawings shown at the end of this chapter depict the earliest instance of a lock-picking gun that the author could find. It was invented by either Nathan Epstein or his brother, Eli Epstein. The drawings present a device that looked vaguely familiar to the author, and it might

have struck some readers that way also. The metal bow
and the flat vibrating spring resemble the Jew's harp, an instrument far more commonplace back then than now. It is
only conjecture that the pick gun was based on the harp,
but one can readily see that the Jew's harp is also an
impact-producing instrument, one which acts horizontally rather than vertically.

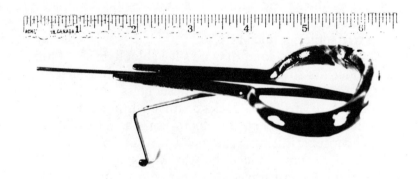

Shown here is a Jew's harp with a second spring of flatwire inserted into
the bow. This spring has a half-turn twist that brings it into vertical relation to the lock tumblers and is kicked upward by fingering the harp's
slide trigger.

This impact-producing device might well have led to the Epstein
pick gun. The Jew's harp was very common in the last century and into
the 1920s. The device in these photos has picked locks, but it could be
made handier with a vertical handgrip.

To test this hypothesis, I procured a harp and inserted into the bow a second, thinner spring of flatwire that was long enough to enter a lock keyway. By pulling back and releasing the mainspring trigger, it would strike the keyway spring and thereby transfer the impact to the pin tumblers. It worked, but was somewhat unwieldy because it didn't have a suitable handgrip.

Mr. Epstein had the quality of mind to discover that impact could be induced within the lock on site, and he went on to fashion a device to accomplish this end—the pick gun.

Who was the real father of the pick gun, Nathan or Eli Epstein? I am indebted to Dan Dwyer (and to the Kellys of Kelly's Locksmithing, who put me in contact with Mr. Dwyer) for much of the information I learned about the Epsteins.

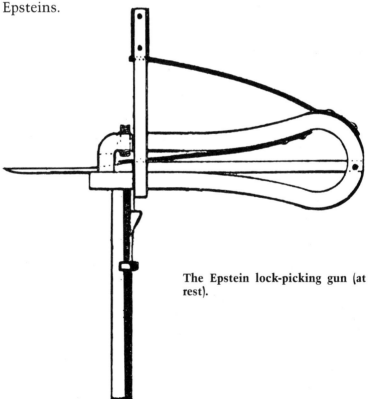

The Epstein lock-picking gun (at rest).

Mr. Dwyer is now in his eighties, but he remembers the Epsteins well. He worked with both "Nate" and Eli in the 1930s and 1940s. Immediately on opening conversation with me, he stated quite categorically that it was Eli and not Nathan who was the inventor of the lock-picking gun (the people at Kelly's Locksmithing in Boston said the same thing), despite the fact that Nathan's name appears on the patent.

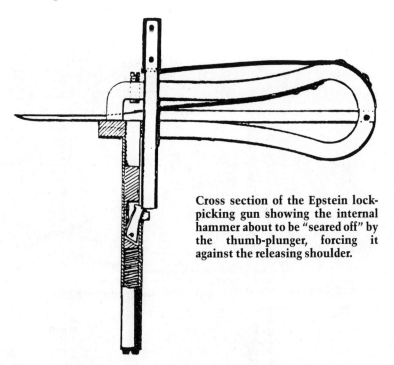

Cross section of the Epstein lock-picking gun showing the internal hammer about to be "seared off" by the thumb-plunger, forcing it against the releasing shoulder.

It seems Eli had quite an inventive turn of mind and, among other things, designed toothpaste tubes and tools for the locksmith trade for which he never received any credit. He made custom key blanks for the large lock-shops, and he had a bench in a room by himself where he worked as a locksmith's locksmith, tackling the difficult work sent to him by other locksmiths. He also worked at many of the larger locksmith and hardware shops, such as

Dougmore & Duncan and Kelly's, and he was employed for a time by the Independent Lock Company in nearby Fitchburg.

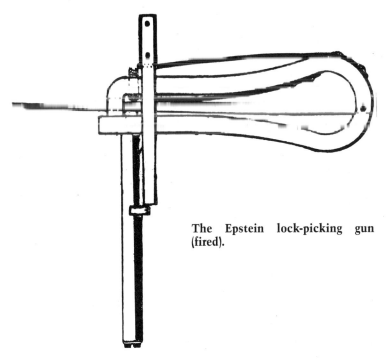

The Epstein lock-picking gun (fired).

Independent Lock was run by the Falks in those days, and Eli married one of the Falk daughters. They had a son, but the marriage didn't work out and they were estranged for many years. The reason for mentioning this family history is that Barney Zion, the subject of the next chapter, was also related by marriage to the Falks. (Mr. Zion was related to the Zions of Montreal, Canada, the founders of Dominion Lock, another famous name in the lock industry.)

Eli Epstein stood only five feet, seven inches, but he was a giant just the same. Not to be eclipsed by his own invention, he also designed a pick-proof lock cylinder before he passed away in the 1940s, according to Dan Dwyer.

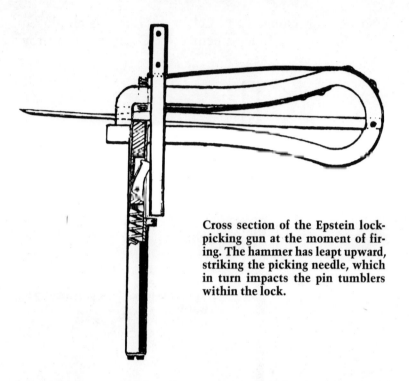

Cross section of the Epstein lock-picking gun at the moment of firing. The hammer has leapt upward, striking the picking needle, which in turn impacts the pin tumblers within the lock.

Mr. Dwyer also told me that the Yale & Towne Company (*the* name in locks) bought the rights to Epstein's lock-picking gun in the twenties in order to keep it off the market, so threatened did they feel by it. And rightly so, since it was such a revolutionary development in lock picking. The construction and function of the lock-picking device is clearly laid out in the patent, so I will not belabor the points here other than to say that it is an easily made item by anyone familiar with metal-working tools, and it is worth the effort to construct.

★ ★ ★ ★ ★ ★ ★

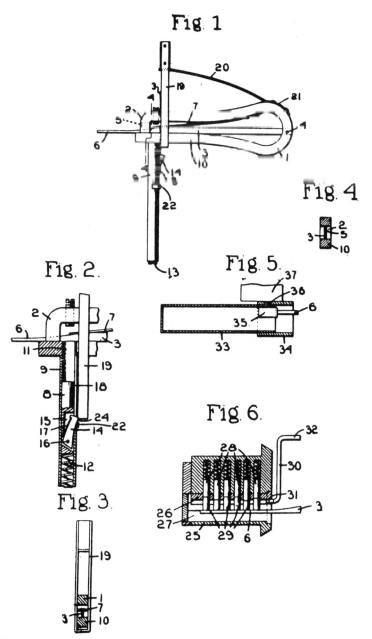

Fig. 1

Fig. 2.

Fig. 3.

Fig. 4

Fig. 5.

Fig. 6.

The Epstein patent.

UNITED STATES PATENT OFFICE

NATHAN EPSTEIN, BOSTON, MASSACHUSETTS

IMPACT-PRODUCING IMPLEMENT

1,403,753 Specification of Letters Patent. Patented Jan. 17, 1922.

Application filed September 28, 1920. Serial No. 413,430.

To all whom it may concern:

Be it known that I, NATHAN EPSTEIN, a citizen of the United States, and a resident of Boston, county of Suffolk, State of Massachusetts, have invented an Improvement in Impact-Producing Implements, of which the following description, in connection with the accompanying drawing, is a specification, like characters on the drawing representing like parts.

This invention has for its object to provide a novel implement designed to produce impacts or hammer-like blows, and which is so constructed that it will deliver said blows within a confined space, as for instance within a small tube or pocket.

A device embodying my invention is capable of a wide range of use, and as illustrating such a wide range, I would state that it is adapted for use as a lock-picking implement, or as an implement for delivering hammer-like blows to a rivet head situated within a tube or other small confined space. Both of these uses are illustrated in the drawings, but they are referred to merely as showing the capacity of the implement for widely different uses, and not for the purpose of in any way limiting the use to which the invention may be put.

My improved implement comprises a frame, which will preferably be constructed so that it can be readily held in the hand, and an impact-delivering member movably connected to the frame and projecting beyond the latter, thereby permitting it to be inserted into the confined space, a spring-impelled or impact-producing member constructed to deliver the hammer-like blows to the impact-delivering element, and means, which is preferably operable by the movement of the thumb or finger of the hand in which the implement is held, for placing the spring of the impact-producing member under tension and then releasing the spring, thereby to deliver the blow.

In order to give an understanding of my invention, I have illustrated in the accompanying drawings some selected embodiments thereof, which will now be described, after which the novel features will be pointed out in the appended claims.

Fig. 1 of the drawings is a side view of the implement embodying my invention.

Fig. 2 is a fragmentary, sectional view on a larger scale, showing the manner in which the spring of the impact-producing element is compressed and then released;

Fig. 3 is a section on the line 3—3, Fig. 1;

Fig. 4 is a section on the line 4—4, Fig. 1;

Fig. 5 is a view showing one way in which the device may be used;

Fig. 6 shows how the device is used as a lock-picking implement.

The implement herein shown comprises a frame 1 which has a general U-shape, the end of one of the arms of the U being bent inwardly toward the other arm, as shown at 2, and constituting a guiding member for the impact-delivering element. This impact-delivering element is herein shown as an arm or lever 3 pivoted to the frame at 4, and extending through a guiding slot 5 formed in the portion 2, said member 3 projecting beyond the frame a considerable distance as shown at 6. The projecting portion 6 of the member 3 constitutes the portion of the device which delivers the impact. The impact-delivering member 3 is acted on by a spring 7 which normally holds it in retracted position.

The end 6 of the member 3 is given its movement to deliver the impact by the operation of a spring-actuated impact-producing element. This impact-producing element is herein shown as a plunger or hammer member 8, which is slidably mounted in the tube 9 secured to and depending from the arm 10 of the frame, said arm having an opening 11 there through in alignment with the tube and forming a continuation of the bore of the tube.

Situated within the tube 9 is a spring 12 which acts on the member 8 and tends to urge it upwardly or towards the impact-delivering member. The lower end of the spring is shown as being situated against a plug 13, which is screwed into the lower end of the tube 9 and is removable therefrom. By removing the plug 13, the spring 12 and plunger 8 can be removed if such action is necessary.

Means are provided for retracting the plunger 8 and compressing the spring 12 and then releasing said spring, so that the expansive movement of the spring will drive the plunger 8 upwardly in the tube and against the member 3 with a hammer-like blow. This will give a quick, impact-delivering movement to the portion 6 of the impact-delivering member 3. For this purpose I have provided a dog 14, which is situated within a slot 15 formed in the plunger 8 and is pivotally mounted thereto as shown at 16, said dog being acted upon by a spring 17 which tends to move it outwardly. The tube 9 is provided with a slot 18 through which the dog normally projects, as shown in Fig. 1.

I have also provided a member 19 which can be operated by the thumb or finger of the hand, and the function of which is to act on the dog 14 and compress the spring 12. This member 19 is in the form of a yoke which embraces the frame, and which is connected at its upper end to a spring arm 20 that is secured to the frame as shown at 21.

The member 19 stands in line with the dog 14, so that when said member 19 is moved downwardly against the action of the spring 20, it will engage the dog and thereby carry the plunger 8 downwardly against the action of the spring 12. When the plunger has been fully retracted, then the dog is automatically released from the member 19, thereby allowing the spring 12 to throw the dog forward with a quick movement. For this purpose, the tube 9 is formed with a dog-releasing member 22 situated at the lower end of the slot 18, and arranged so that when the back side 24 of the dog engages the member 22, as shown in Fig. 2, a further downward movement of the dog will cam said dog inwardly out of the path of movement of the member 19, thus disengaging the dog from the member 19.

As soon as this has occurred, the spring 12 will automatically expand, thus throwing the plunger 8 forward with a quick movement, and causing it to strike the member 3 with a hammer-like blow. This blow will produce in the member 3 a quick, hammer-like movement the extent of which is limited by the slot 5, and during such movement the spring 7 will be compressed. The spring 7 is a relatively light spring whose only function is to restore the member 3 to its normal position after the blow has been delivered, and therefore the said spring has no appreciable effect in retarding the hammer-like blow of the impact-delivering member 3.

As soon as the member 19 has been depressed to a point sufficient to release the dog, then said member is released and returned to its normal position by the action of spring 20.

The frame is of such a shape that it can be conveniently held in the hand, and the member 19 can conveniently be depressed by the action of the thumb or one of the fingers.

One use to which the invention is especially adapted is that of picking so-called cylinder locks, and in Fig. 6, I have illustrated the manner in which the device can be used for this purpose. In said figure, 25 indicates the cylinder of a cylinder lock, 26 indicates the plug having the key slot 27,

28 indicates the spring-pressed tumbler pins carried by the cylinder 25, and 29 indicates the drivers that are actuated when the key is inserted.

One familiar way of picking a lock of this type is to jar the barrel repeatedly and at the same time apply a slight pressure to the plug, the jarring operation resulting in driving the tumbler pins 28 backwardly against the action of their springs. A continued jarring will eventually line up all of the tumbler pins so that the plug can be turned.

In using my device for picking a lock, the projection portion 6 of the impact delivering member 3 is inserted in the key slot 27 beneath the drivers 29, and then the device is operated thereby to give impacts to the drivers. This results in driving the tumbler pins backwardly against the action of the spring, and by exerting a slight pressure on the plug during this operation, any tumbler pin that is driven back completely out of the plug 26 will be held in such position so long as the pressure is applied. By delivering the repeated impacts against the drivers, it is possible to line up all of the tumbler pins, thereby unlocking the plug so that it can be turned.

The pressure may be applied to the plug in various ways while the impacts are being delivered. One way would be by using an implement 30 in the form of a crank, one end 31 of which is inserted into the upper end of the key slot, and the other end 32 of which constitutes a finger-piece by which turning pressure may be applied to the plug. The shape of the impact-producing implement is such that it can operate on a cylinder lock while the latter is in the door, so that this invention provides a device by which a cylinder lock can be readily picked without removing it from the door.

Another use to which the invention is especially applicable is illustrated in Fig. 5, wherein 33 indicates a tube having one end inserted into a sleeve or tube 34 and which it is desired to rivet to the sleeve 34. When the implement is to be used for this purpose, the projecting end 6 of the impact-delivering member will preferably be formed with

The Father of the Pick Gun   25

a hammer-head 35 of a size that it can be inserted into the tube 33—34. After the rivet 36 is inserted, then the outer end of the rivet may be held against an anvil 37 and the hammer-head 35 introduced within the sleeves. By actuating the implement, the hammer-head will give the inner end of the rivet repeated blows sufficient to upset the end of the rivet, and thus rivet the two tubes together.

The above are only two suggestions as to uses to which the invention may be put, and I wish it understood that the invention in capable of a variety of other uses.

I claim:

1. In an impact-producing implement, the combination with a frame having a guide, of an impact-delivering member movably mounted on said frame, a relatively light spring acting against said member in opposition to its impact-delivering movement, a spring-actuated impact-producing member slidable in said guide and adapted to strike the impact-delivery member a hammer-like blow, and a reciprocating actuator adapted during its movement to engage the impact-producing member, thereby to compress its spring and then to release said member to permit the spring to act.

2. In an impact-producing implement, the combination with a frame, of an impact-delivering member pivotally mounted thereon, a relatively light spring acting against said impact-delivering movement, a spring-actuated impact-producing member adapted to strike the impact-delivering member a hammer-like blow, a dog carried by the impact-producing, and an actuator arranged to engage the dog and thereby compress the spring of the impact-producing member, and then to release the dog to permit said spring to act.

3. In an impact-producing implement, the combination with a frame constructed to be held in the hand and having a tubular guiding member extending laterally therefrom, of an impact-delivering member pivoted to the frame and extending beyond the latter, a spring-actuated impact-producing member slidably mounted in said tube,

the latter being slotted, a dog carried by said impact-producing member and operating in said slot, and an actuator arranged to engage the dog and thereby move the impact-producing member backwardly against the spring, and means for releasing the dog from said actuator.

4. In an impact-producing implement, the combination with a frame constructed to be held in the hand, and having a tubular guiding portion extending laterally therefrom, of an impact-delivering member pivoted to the frame and extending beyond the latter, a relatively light spring acting against said impact-delivering member in opposition to its impact-delivering movement, an impact-producing member slidably mounted in the tube, the latter having a slot, a dog pivoted to the impact-producing member and extending through the slot, a spring acting on said impact-producing member, and an actuating member movably carried by the frame and adapted to engage said dog, thereby to compress said spring, and means for automatically releasing the dog from said actuator when the spring is compressed, so that the latter will cause the impact-producing member to deliver a hammer-like blow against the impact-delivering member.

In testimony whereof I have signed my name to this specification.

NATHAN EPSTEIN

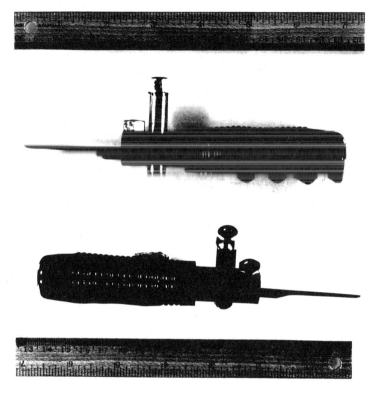

The author's version of the Epstein patent. The vertical plunger is a tube slotted along three-fourths of its length to allow the pick needle to be centered and slid within. Directly above the needle in the tube is a compression spring held in by the end cap. By pressing with the thumb downward against this cap, the tube extends beneath the pipe body and jumps upward when released, immediately striking the pick needle just as in Epstein's original patent. The forward grab screw and lock nut are for adjusting the impact stroke.

Chapter Three

Mr. Majestic

Bernard "Barney" Zion was born in 1887. He went to work for the Independent Lock Company in 1928, earning a commission of fifty dollars for every machine he sold. He was a good salesman but he wanted to own his own business, so with little money down, he founded the Majestic Lock Company in 1931. He had a four-room office next to the Woolworth Building, off lower Broadway in Manhattan. It was a small business, employing Barney, his wife, and his assistant, Dick Feingold.

In 1931, Barney invented the Lockaid pick gun and by 1935 had a patent claim filed. He became one of the better-known New York locksmiths of his day and worked closely with the police department and federal agencies. During World War II, he tutored informal classes for intelligence agents going overseas to prepare them for the types of locks they might encounter there.

The Lockaid pick gun was closely controlled by the authorities, and each one was registered and sold only to locksmiths and police officials. The guns traditionally came in wooden boxes of dovetailed construction, with detailed instructions on how to use the device. The early guns were made of a much heavier gauge steel than what

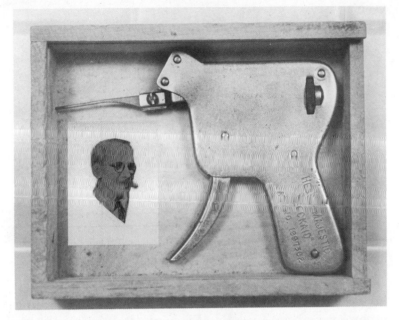

Mr. Majestic, Bernard "Barney" Zion, and his Lockaid pick gun, Pat. No. 1,997,362. This gun belonged to an FBI agent. It was made in the 1940s and is noticeably heavier than modern lock-pick guns. Note the riveted construction and wooden issue box.

is currently used. The guns resembled toy cap guns and were riveted closed. They were guaranteed for life and, if anything went wrong, it was only necessary to return them for repair. The author had occasion to use this service and was quite impressed by it.

The Epstein patent had run out by the 1930s, and everyone was free to manufacture his own version of the gun. Yet the Majestic Lockaid pick gun brought the "impact-producing implement" to its highest functional form. It felt good in the user's hand, and Barney Zion also claimed his gun imparted control and "touch" to picking.

Hardly ever without a cigar and always surrounded by dossiers of key codes, Barney Zion was a real character and a legend in American locksmithing. Every locksmith worthy of the name has owned a Lockaid pick gun at one time or another, and sometimes several—one for the

The Lockaid pick gun complete with box and instructions.

bench, one for the truck, and one for spare. It is hard to im-
agine working without one.

* * * * * * *

There are a few modifications that can be done to the
Lockaid pick gun to improve its performance or to suit the
individual tastes of the user.

First, I never liked the grip. It is vestigal at best, and
should be lengthened to give the gun more control. This is
perhaps best accomplished by affixing sideplates (like the
ones on a regular pistol) so that they extend downward at
least a finger width. These can be fashioned out of wood or
plastic.

Second, the trigger can be shortened as an alternative to
the original pick gun, or as an adjunct modification. Most
users will be strong enough to achieve the same trigger
pull and would prefer to have the gun fill their hand more
fully than the present size.

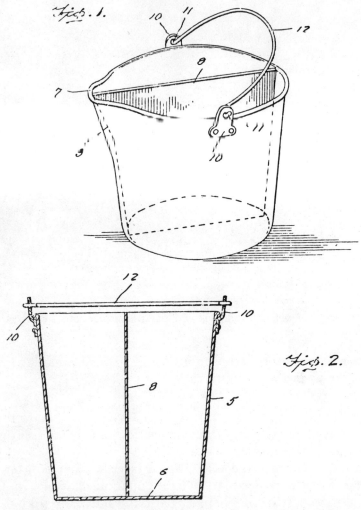

Fig. 1.

Fig. 2.

The patent number on the grip of the Majestic Lockaid pick gun is 1,997,362. The U.S. Patent Office, however, has this dual-compartment bucket registered under that particular number. It appears to have been placed on the pick guns to prevent duplication rather than for patent protection.

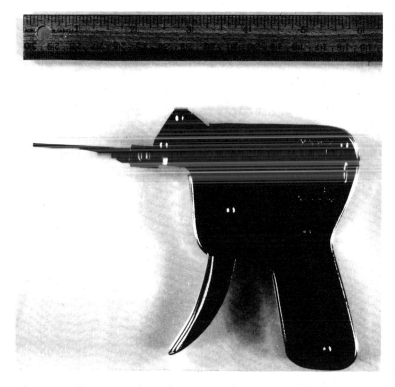

The E-Z Pick Gun. Made in the Orient, these guns sell for about one-third the price of the Majestic.

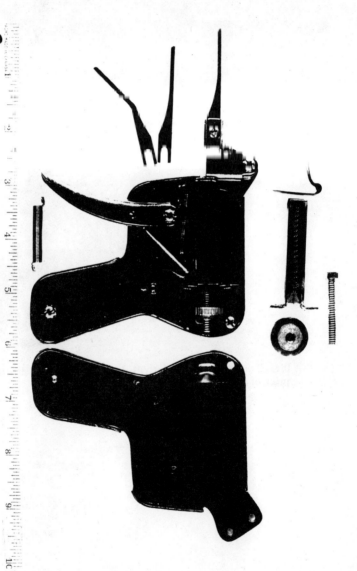

The guts of the E-Z Pick Gun show a large trigger, "V" lever, spring-loaded hammer, and impact-adjusting wheel. The pick-needle holder resembles a boxer's arm cocked at the elbow.

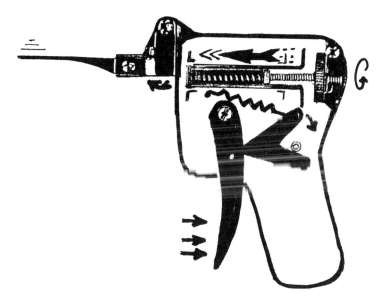

This diagram shows the E-Z Pick Gun at the instant of hammer release. The "V" sear has dropped downward as the trigger has drawn the spring-loaded hammer rearward. It is flying forward to hit the pick-needle swing arm at its elbow. This movement, in turn, impacts on the pin tumblers within the lock.

As with regular pistols, this gun should also have a holster. This would make the gun easier to carry and at the same time would protect the delicate needle pick, which forever snags in pockets. The holster can be worn on the belt and can also hold spare needles and tension wrenches in a side pocket, similar to European military or police holsters.

The attachment of the needles to the gun is another sore point for me. They can come loose at the most inopportune times, but this can be alleviated by the use of a miniature wing nut, which will allow the tightening of the clamp.

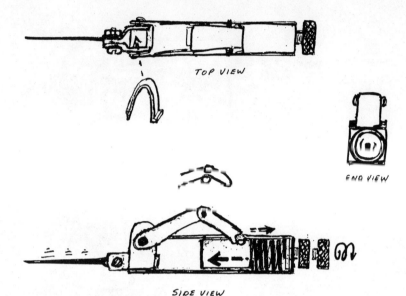

TOP VIEW

END VIEW

SIDE VIEW

The Click-it is a compact version of the E-Z Pick Gun. It is triggered by pressing down with the thumb on the toggle joint. This device was designed by the author and called "The Click-it" because it resembles a cricket or grasshopper.

Don't be afraid to make your own needles out of spring stock. The notches can be cut with small-diameter chainsaw files or Dremel-tool abrasive wheels. You can also make needles having sinous (wavy) pick patterns as well as half-diamond patterns so that you can use the pick gun as an ordinary pick when locks don't respond to the vibrations. Extreme paracentric keyways may require very narrow or thin picks, so you also should have some of those on hand.

★ ★ ★ ★ ★ ★ ★

F.B.I. LOCK-RELEASE GUN INSTRUCTIONS FOR THE LOCKAID PICK GUN

Since locks with the pin-tumbler embodiment are the most widely used, the attached sketches will help you operate the Lock Gun.

The Lock Release Gun is not an automatic instrument that opens locks by mere trigger action. It will open locks easily only when properly used.

Both hands are required to open locks with this instrument. A small black tension wrench is supplied with each gun. Do not attempt to open locks without this wrench.

Pin-tumbler-type locks have a cylinder core or round shaft that rotates to the left (counterclockwise) or right (clockwise) after inserting a key in the keyway in the center of this cylinder core or shaft is the keyhole or keyway, which is an oblong slit in a vertical position (see Figure 1).

When opening this type of lock with a regular key, first insert the key, turn the key to the right or left, and the lock is opened. By inserting the key and *not turning it,* the lock will never open.

It is the same with the Lock Gun. After inserting the gun needle in the keyway and pulling the trigger, the lock will not open unless the keyway turns to the right or left. Since the needle would break if you tried to turn the keyway, it's necessary to use the small tension wrench at this point.

When you trigger the gun, the upward blows of the needle knocks the tumblers in place so the shaft or cylinder core will turn freely and open the latch. The turning of the shaft or core when using the lock gun is done by turning the tension wrench.

Before attempting to open a lock with the gun, determine whether the keyway turns to the right or left. A good many tumbler locks turn either way to open. Others turn only to the right, while others go to the left.

It is safe to assume that the keyway should be turned to the right. If this does not work, use the tension wrench so the keyway turns to the left.

Step-by-Step Procedure
1. A knurled wheel at the back of the gun takes care of the tension adjustment of the blow. The wheel is

turned toward you for greater tension, and away from you for less tension. Before starting to work on a lock, turn the wheel away from you as far as it will go. Then turn the wheel toward you five turns, which will produce a little tension.

2. First insert one curved end of the tension wrench at the bottom of the keyway. Arrange one curved end of the wrench in the keyway so the other end will hang slightly to the left. In this position, the wrench will act as a lever, permitting you to turn the core after the tumblers are knocked into place.

3. Insert the gun needle in the keyway directly above the end of the wrench. Keep the needle as low as possible in the keyway under the tumbler pins. When inserting the gun needle, keep it in a straight line—just remember how straight a regular key fits into a keyhole. Don't push the gun needle into the keyway too far. Glance at one of your keys. The notches should give you an idea of how far to insert the needle. Inserting the needle too far will catch the inside end of the lock and fail to strike the pins.

4. While holding the gun free in the lock with one hand, maintain a slight pressure on the wrench with a finger of your left hand. Only a slight touch on the wrench is necessary. Don't jerk or exert heavy pressure on the wrench.

5. Pull the trigger while holding the gun needle in a straight line and pull slowly. After each shot, apply a slight finger pressure to the wrench with your left finger. Then release the finger pressure on the wrench.

6. When the gun needle knocks the pins into position inside the lock, you will feel a slight "give" on the wrench. This means the gun has done its work and you should immediately stop triggering. Turn the wrench slowly to the right as you would a key and the shaft will turn and open the lock.

7. By using the wrench as a lever, push your finger to the

right. The keyway will turn with the wrench and the lock will open.

8. It is going to be slightly awkward to keep the curved end of the wrench in place in the bottom of the keyway without using too much pressure with your finger or fingers. However, after a few trials, this awkwardness will disappear.

9. Try both curved ends in the bottom of the keyway. One end is slightly narrower than the other.

10. The wrench can also be used at the top of the keyway, but this is more awkward.

11. If the lock does not open after eight or nine shots, release the tension on the wrench, allowing the pins to drop back into place, and start over. If the lock still does not open, keep turning the wheel of the gun toward you for more tension. Keep a record of the number of turns it takes to successfully open a lock, as this will serve as a guide for similar locks.

12. Some locks have narrow corrugated keyways, which means that the gun blade or needle will have to be filed thinner. Never file the top edge of the blade or needle—file only the sides or bottom.

13. An additional offset gun needle is furnished with each gun. This is used only on locks that are directly on top of the doorknob, in which case the needle cannot be held in the keyway in a straight line.

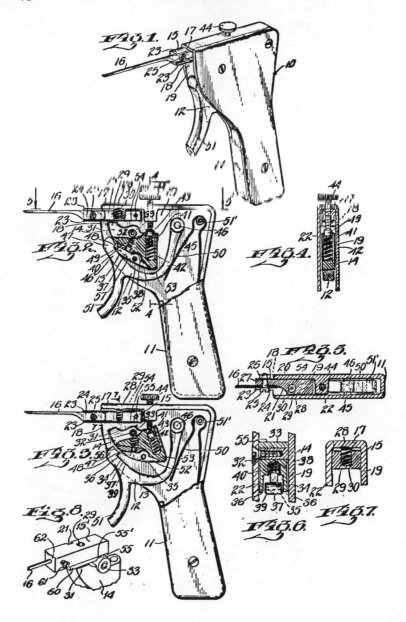

The Segal patent.

Chapter Four

The Segal Patent

UNITED STATES PATENT OFFICE

SAMUEL SEGAL, BROOKLYN, NEW YORK

LOCK-PICKING GUN

2,309,677. Specification of Letters Patent.
Application filed May 5, 1939. Serial No. 271,996.

The present invention is directed to an impact-producing implement and more particularly is concerned with a functionally and structurally improved serviceable lock-pick gun and the objects, advantages, and features thereof will be apparent from the teachings of the following detailed description viewed in the light of the accompanying drawing wherein:

Fig. 1 is a perspective view of the lock-pick gun according to my invention.

Fig. 2 is a front elevational view of Fig. 1 with parts

broken away to show the internal construction.

Fig. 3 is a view similar to Fig. 2, however illustrating the impact-delivering rocking arm in a released position and ready to impart a blow to the vertically shiftable lock-pick shoe or holder.

Fig. 4 is a sectional view on the line 4—4 of Fig. 2.

Fig. 5 is a horizontal section view on the line 5—5 of Fig. 2.

Fig. 6 is a sectional view taken on the line 6—6 of Fig. 3.

Fig. 7 is a sectional view on the line 7—7 of Fig. 3, and

Fig. 8 is a perspective view of a modified form of the shoe and support.

Illustrative of the embodiment disclosed, the lock-pin gun is generated denoted 10 and compromises a hollow metal casing 11, a pivoted trigger 12, a trigger-locking pawl or dog 13 pivotally mounted on the pivoted impact-delivery rocking arm or hammer 14, a vertically and bodily shiftable lock-pick holder or shoe 15, and the lock pick 16.

According to the invention, shoe 15 is vertically guided between upper and lower stops 17 and 18 integral with the back wall 19 of the casing by a key or rib 20 projecting from wall 19. More particularly, rib 20 cooperates with the spaced transverse walls of the vertical keyway or slot 21 in the shoe to vertically and slidably guide the shoe between the back wall or plate 19 and the cover 22 of the case.

The shoe or pick holder 15 is provided with upper and lower flanges 23 defining a channel in which the expanded part 24 of the pick is inserted and clamping means in the form of a bolt 25, and nut 26 is utilized to hold the expanded part 24 firmly against the reduced part 27 of the shoe, which overhangs the forward end of the casing. In the normal or retracted position of the trigger (Fig. 1), the shoe 15 is also in a retracted or elevated position; namely, the upper flange 23 together with the upper face of the shoe are against the upper stop 17, which serves as the top wall of the casing.

In such retracted relation of the shoe, it will be observed that the lower flange 23 is spaced or away from the lower stop or seat 16. Cap or tumbler 28, which is telescopically slidable in bore 29 of the rear part of shoe 15 and which is now against the stop 17, compresses the helicoidal spring 30 in that the hammer portion 31 of the impact-delivering device 14 is in its fully raised position and abutting the lower flange 23 of the shoe, thus supporting the latter.

The impact-delivering device 14 includes the transversely arranged bore 32 receiving the fixed fulcrum post 33, which extends from the rear wall of the casing. By thin arrangement, the impact-delivering device is pivotally or rotatably mounted on the fulcrum post 33. The impact-delivering device also includes a recess 34, which is bridged by the fixed fulcrum post 35 secured to sides 36 of recess 34, which sides serve to tiltably guide pawl 13 pivotally sustained by post 35.

The latch or pawl 13 has its longest arm 37 normally urged outwardly by reason of the helicoidal spring 38, in part encompassing a post 39 fixed to arm 37 and in part projecting into a recess 40 in the impact-delivering device or rotatable lever 14, which is provided with a bore 41 housing the normally expanded spring 42 surrounding the reduced stem of the slidable tumbler 43 telescopically receivable in bore 41.

For controlling the power of the impact to be struck by hammer portion 31 of the impact-delivery device 14 against shoe 15, means has been provided for adjusting the power spring 42. To this end a threaded set screw 44 is employed. This set screw is threadably connected to stop 17 and to a depending lug integral with the stop and cooperates with the slidable tumbler 43 to regulate the desired kickback power in the spring 42.

As previously set forth, the trigger 12 is normally in a retracted position as shown in Fig. 2. This trigger has one arm 45 pivoted on the fixed fulcrum post 46 fixedly carried by the rear wall of the casing. Another arm 46' of the trigger is provided with a nose or lip portion 47 having an inclined-actuating shoulder or projecting catch 48 disposed in close proximity to end face 49 of the long arm 37 of pivoted pawl 15. As shown in Fig. 2 of the forward end of trigger 12, which is normally held in a retracted position by reason of reach 50 of the inverted U-shaped leaf spring 51' appropriately retained within the casing, is interlocked with the forward end of the pawl; that is, end face 49 of the pawl cooperates with shoulder 48 of the trigger to lock the latter against involuntary rearward displacement. If, therefore, the finger-gripping portion 51 of the trigger is moved rearwardly, the trigger is caused to pivot rearwardly against the resistance of reach 50.

During this operation, shoulder 48 abuts the end face 19 of the pawl, thus bodily shifting the latter rearwardly and, since the tapered tail or short arm 52 of the pawl is against the inclined face 53 of the rockable hammer or impact-delivering device 14, the latter is pivoted bodily or counterclockwise. Thus the hammer portion 31 of the hammer or the impact-delivering device 14 is moved away from the shoe 15 and the latter drops by gravity on the lower stop 18 and such action is accelerated by the expansion of spring 30 once the shoe 15 loses the support of the hammer. To resist tilting of the shoe 15 after the support of the hammer 14 has been removed, the rear end of the shoe has a projection 54 cooperating with the curved stop or seat 55 to limit downward displacement; that is, the shoe drops vertically at the beginning of an operative cycle, which starts to take place at the beginning of the rearward stroke of the trigger, thus causing the upper flange 23 of the shoe to fall away from stop 17.

As the cycle continues, the trigger continues to travel rearwardly and lip 48 continues to abut the latch, which in turn causes the impact-producing device to rotate or pivot rearwardly, that is, counterclockwise, at which time the helicoidal power spring 42 becomes compressed in that the shank of the set screw 44 forces the slidable tumbler into bore 41.

The impact-producing device or hammer 14 rotates rearwardly until lip 47 of the trigger slips off from the end face 49 of the nose of the long arm 37 of the pawl 13. Thus the trigger becomes free of the pawl in which instant the power spring releases its energy and expands, thus causing the impact-producing device to retract in a clockwise direction whereby the hammer portion 31 imparts an appreciable impact and shock against the lower flange 23 of the shoe 15, which is abruptly lifted or raised from its stops or seats 18 and 55 and against the energy spring 30 to abruptly position the upper flange 23 of the shoe against the stop 17. In other words, a sudden blow is imparted by the hammer portion to the shoe and consequently the pick thereof is also bodily lifted.

With the impact-producing device 14 automatically restored to its normal position (Fig. 2), the trigger is also retracted automatically upon release of finger pressure on the manipulating portion 51, in which instant reach 50 of the leaf spring 51' urges the trigger forwardly. On the retraction of the trigger, cam face 56 of the lip 47 contacts the bottom curved face 57 of the pivoted pawl 13, thus causing the long arm 37 of the latter to be rocked into the recess 34 against the action of spring 38 to permit lip 47 of the trigger to pass the nose or front end of the pawl, after which spring 33 expands, causing the arm 37 of the pawl to move outwardly again and interlock with lip 47, thus ending a complete cycle of operation and the trigger is again in its normal and waiting relation.

It follows, therefore, that on each cycle of operation, the lock pick drops against the lower stop as the trigger starts to recede, the hammer begins to pivot rearwardly, the power spring starts to store a certain amount of energy until the pawl becomes free of the lip of the trigger, at which time the power spring suddenly dissipates its energy and the hammer automatically retracts to strike the shoe carrying the lock pick. Therefore the latter is elevated against the upper stop. Following this impact, the trigger retracts automatically to interlock with the pawl. Thus by the present arrangement, a certain vibratory motion is imparted to the pick when the trigger is snapped through several cycles. The lifting impact to the pick is utilized to control certain tumblers of a conventional cylinder lock (not shown); that is, in the matter of picking the latter. The lifting impact applied to the tumblers is transmitted to the drivers of the cylinder lock for parting the latter from the tumblers. Once this is established, the cylinder lock is picked. This is in line with the well-known principles of picking cylinder locks and further discussion in respect to the method of picking locks therefore need not be further discussed.

The shoe 15' according to the showing of Fig. 8 is provided with bore 62 for receiving the rear end of the pick 16, which is adjustably held clamped by the set screw 61. Attached to the bottom face of the shoe 15' is the block 60, which is of a suitable sound-deadening material. This block is provided with an arcuate shoulder 55' cooperating with the curved stop 55 to prevent tilting of the shoe when hammer portion 31 of the rockable lever 14 is operated. In other structural aspects, the form according to Fig. 8 is along the lines of the emodiment according to Fig. 1.

Without further analysis, the foregoing disclosure will so fully reveal the gist of the present invention that others may, by applying current knowledge, readily adapt it to various applications without omitting certain features, that from the standpoint of the prior art, fairly constitute the essential characteristics of the generic and special aspects of the invention and therefore such adaptations should and are intended to be comprehended within the meaning and range of equivalency of the following claims:

I claim:

1. In an impact-delivering device, a casing having upper and lower stops, a vertically displaceable shoe movable between said stops, a pick carried by said shoe and extending laterally of said casing, a pivoted hammer within said casing and having a shoulder, a power helicoidal spring within said hammer, adjustable means carried by said casing and cooperating with said spring for holding said hammer against said shoe to normally hold the latter against said upper stop, a pawl pivoted to said hammer and having

a forward portion, spring means normally urging said forward portion of said pawl out of said hammer, a trigger pivotally sustained within said casing and having a catch, a leaf spring for normally holding said catch to interlock with said portion, and a manipulator carried by said trigger for operating the latter to shift said pawl to rearwardly and pivotally displace said hammer away from said shoe whereby the latter falls by gravity against said lower stop and whereby said adjustable means compresses said power spring until said shoulder is free of said forward portion of said pawl

2. In an impact-delivering device, a casing having upper and lower stops, a vertically displaceable shoe movable between said stops, a relatively thin pick carried by said shoe and extending laterally of said casing, a pivoted hammer sustained by and within said casing, a power helicoidal spring within said hammer, adjustable means carried by said casing and cooperating with said spring for holding said hammer against said shoe to normally hold the latter against said upper stop, a pawl pivoted to said hammer and having a terminal, spring means for projecting said terminal out of said hammer, a trigger pivotally sustained within said casing and having a shoulder, an inverted U-shaped leaf spring for normally holding said trigger to removably engage said terminal and shoulder, and a manipulator carried by said trigger and disposed outside of said casing to shift said pawl to rearwardly and pivotally displace said hammer away from said shoe whereby the latter falls by gravity against said lower stop and whereby said adjustable means compresses said power spring until said shoulder is free of said terminal, at which time said leaf spring automatically retracts said trigger to tiltably shift said terminal of said pawl within the hammer to permit said shoulder to pass said terminal whereupon said spring means urges said terminal outwardly to engage with said shoulder.

3. In an impact-delivering device, a casing having upper and lower stops, a vertically displaceable shoe movable be-

tween said stops, a relatively thin pick carried by said shoe
and extending laterally of said casing, a pivoted hammer
sustained by and within said casing and including a stop
at the rear thereof, a power helicoidal spring within said
hammer, adjustable means carried by said casing and cooperating with said spring for holding said hammer
against said shoe to normally hold the latter against said
upper stop, a pawl pivoted to said hammer and including a
tail, spring means for projecting a forward portion of said
pawl out of said hammer and said tail against said stop of
said hammer, a trigger pivoted within said casing and having a catch, an inverted U-shaped leaf spring for normally
holding said catch to interlock with said forward portion,
and a manipulator carried by said trigger and disposed outside of said casing for displacing said trigger to shift said
pawl rearwardly to rearwardly and pivotally displace said
hammer away from said shoe whereby the latter falls by
gravity against said lower stop and whereby said adjustable means compresses said power spring until said trigger
is free of said forward portion, at which time said leaf
spring automatically retracts said trigger to tiltably shift
said forward portion of said pawl within the hammer and
said tail away from said stop of said hammer to permit said
catch to pass the forward portion, whereupon said spring
means urges said forward portion outwardly of said hammer to interlock with said catch.

4. In an impact-delivering device, a casing having upper
and lower stops, a vertically displaceable shoe movable between said stops, a relatively thin pick carried by said shoe
and extending laterally of said casing, a pivoted hammer
sustained by and within said casing and including an inclined stop at the rear thereof, a power helicoidal spring
within said hammer adjustable means carried by said casing and co-operating with said spring for holding said hammer against said shoe to normally hold the latter against
said upper stop, a pawl pivoted to said hammer and including a tail, spring means for projecting a forward portion of
said pawl out of said hammer and said tail against said in-

clined stop, a trigger pivotally sustained within said casing
and including a shoulder at its forward end, an inverted U-
shaped leaf spring for normally holding said trigger to removably engage said forward portion, and a manipulator
carried by said trigger and disposed outside of said casing
for shifting said shoulder against said forward portion of
said pawl to rearwardly and pivotally displace said hammer away from said shoe whereby the latter falls by gravity against said lower stop and whereby said adjustable
means compresses said power spring until said shoulder is
free of said forward portion, at which time said leaf spring
automatically and bodily retracts said trigger to tiltably
shift said forward portion of said pawl within the hammer
to permit said shoulder to pass by said forward part of said
pawl, whereupon said spring means urges said forward portion outwardly to interlock with said shoulder.

5. In an impact-delivering device, a casing having upper
and lower stops, a vertically displaceable shoe movable between said stops, a relatively thin pick carried by said shoe
and extending laterally of said casing and having a depending portion, a pivoted hammer sustained by and within
said casing and including a curved stop, a power helicoidal
spring within said hammer, a cap mounted on said spring,
adjustable means carried by said casing and including a depending portion cooperating with said cap to compress
said spring for holding said hammer against said shoe to
normally hold the latter against said upper stop, a pawl
pivoted to said hammer, spring means for projecting a forward portion of said pawl out of said hammer, a trigger
pivoted within said casing and having a projection, an inverted U-shaped leaf spring for normally holding said projection to removably engage said portion, and a manipulator carried by said trigger and disposed outside of said
casing for shifting said trigger and said pawl to rearwardly
and pivotally displace said hammer away from said shoe
whereby the latter falls by gravity against said lower stop
and against said curved stop and whereby said adjustable
means compresses said power spring until said projection

is free of said forward portion, at which time said leaf
spring automatically retracts said trigger to tiltably shift
said forward portion of said pawl within the hammer to
permit to pass said forward portion of said pawl, whereupon said spring means urges said forward portion outwardly to interlock with said projection.

6. In an impact-delivering device, a casing having upper
and lower stops, a vertically displaceable shoe movable between said stops, a pick carried by said shoe and extending
laterally of said casing, a spring controlled tumbler vertically slidable within said shoe and cooperating with said
upper stop, a pivoted hammer within said casing, a power
helicoidal spring within said hammer, adjustable means
carried by said casing and cooperating with said spring for
holding said hammer against said shoe to normally hold
the latter against said upper stop, a pawl carried by said
hammer, spring means normally urging a forward portion
of said pawl out of said hammer, a trigger pivotally sustained within said casing and including a projecting catch,
a leaf spring for normally holding said catch to displace-
ably interlock with said portion, and a manipulator carried by said trigger for operating the latter to shift said
pawl to rearwardly and pivotally displace said hammer
away from said shoe, whereby the latter falls against said
lower stop and whereby the adjustable means compresses
said power spring until said trigger is free of the forward
portion of said pawl.

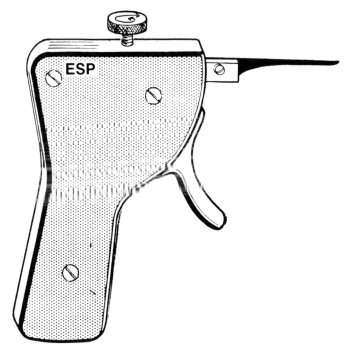

The ESP version of the Segal lock-picking gun. The author has seen
criminally made versions of this gun.

Chapter Five

Genesis of a Pick Gun

In late 1979, I conceived of a wire-pick gun that could be made in a few minutes by using the most ubiquitous of materials—the common coat hanger.

The coat hanger is a drawn-and-formed steel wire about a tenth of an inch thick. It is not a spring, but the metal is snappy enough due to the drawing process.

I cut off the hook and its wire-wound neck and straightened out the coat hanger. A loop was needed, so I secured another common item—a broom handle. After I wrapped the wire a turn and a half around this form, I fashioned a grip and a frame by using two pairs of pliers to bend and twist the wire until I came up with the outline of the wire-pick gun.

The pick-needle portion of the coat-hanger wire was compacted with heavy blows on both sides with a hammer. This densified the metal and forged it into a flattened blade. The now too wide blade was then ground to the shape of the pick needle used on the Lockaid tool.

I immediately tried my creation in the Weiser lock I had on the workbench. It picked after a few snaps of the trigger. The trigger was pulled back and down by the trigger finger and then released. The distance of the pull could be varied

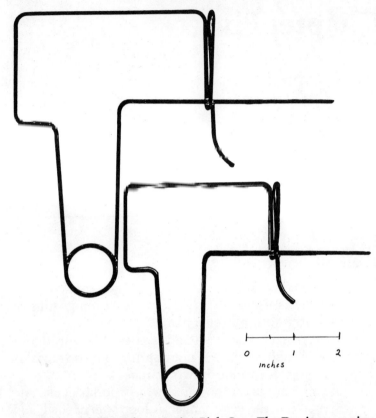

Two versions of the author's Spring Pick Gun. The Derringer version below is designed for handiness—it may be carried in a shirt pocket. They are both made of coat-hanger wire. The S.P.G.-1, available from Hardware Products Corporation (H.P.C.), is a commercially available version of the Spring Pick Gun.

and, therefore, so could the impact on the pin tumblers.

Seeing the success with the Weiser, I then tried a Dominion lock cylinder and then a Schlage key-in-the-knob lock. These, too, were picked in short order. I knew I was on to something then. For the price of a coat hanger, a pick gun was fashioned that could duplicate the action of expensive custom-made tools. It was flimsy to be sure, but if one treated it with care it could simplify the job of emergency picking when one's tools were back at home or at the shop. I called my device the Spring Pick Gun.

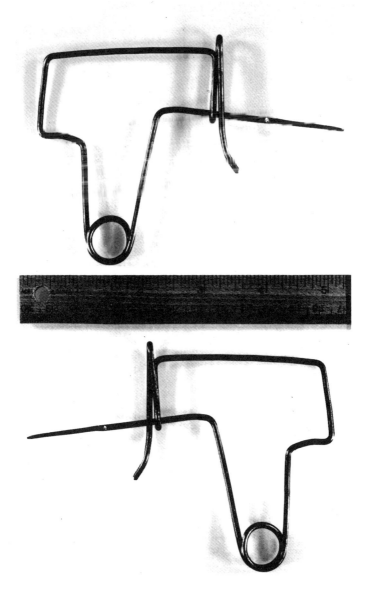

Two Spring Pick Derringers made by the author.

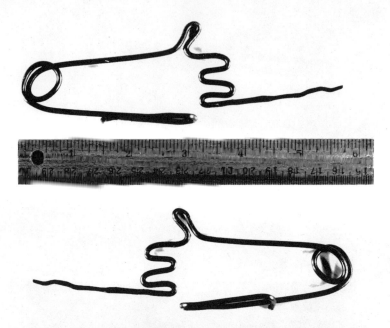

The Spring Pick Ferret, made by the author out of coat-hanger wire. By squeezing the Ferret's body, the lower arm rakes across the twin protuberances, causing the pick needle to vibrate upward and downward as well as forward and backward. The needle is snake-shaped to take advantage of this action. It picks by combined action rather than relying on impact alone. The "ear" of the Ferret is a thumb rest.

I immediately wanted to share my design with other locksmiths, so I sent the design, a sample, and a short description of its manufacture and use to a national locksmith publication. The written comments were published, but not with an accompanying drawing or photo. The article was rendered useless by this oversight, and I felt somewhat miffed that a useful design for a locksmithing tool had been shoved aside.

Having been bitten by the bug to make wire-pick guns, however, I proceeded to make a couple dozen. These were all made by hand at first, but I later designed a template with pins at the appropriate locations.

I had occasion to visit a former CIA man that spring and

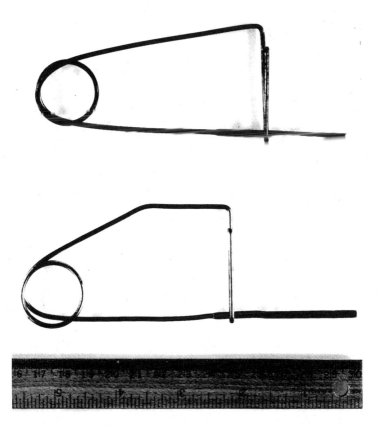

The Lock Clicker. The author remembers this instrument being offered for sale to private detectives in the 1950s.

This device is held in the palm of the hand. Its upper arm is pressed and released by the thumb in a snappy manner. This causes the arm's lower portion, which wraps around the pick needle, to impact against the needle on its return stroke, kicking it upward and transmitting force to the pin tumblers within the lock.

The upper Lock Clicker was made by the author. Note that the needle has been reground. The lower one is commercially available from law enforcement supply houses. It is often illustrated in catalogs being held, incorrectly, upside down.

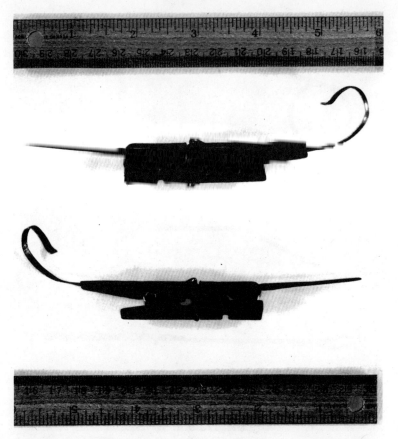

The Scorpion lock clicker is, quite obviously, a clothespin with a channel grooved in it to accept a pin needle made from a street-sweeper brush. The "tail" of the Scorpion curls back and around the user's thumb, and the snap action is provided by the index finger slipping off the lower half of the clothespin after it is pinched together.

took a Spring Pick Gun with me. He was quite enthralled by its design and encouraged me to see if I could find a way to market it. I told him about my experience with the locksmith magazine and said I was not so hopeful, as my article hadn't elicited any inquiries.

This Flare Gun pick has a slip trigger that fires when the thumb slips from the cocking groove. The gun has a tiny hole drilled through its upper body and a flat-spring needle doubled over at the rear for jam fit. It is held vertically in the hand and cocked and released rapidly, causing impact and recoil to transmit along the length of the needle. The gun is made by the Life Support Technology Company of Beaverton, Oregon.
Note: The expended flare cartridge is cut down for clearance.

Later that year, I attended the Master Locksmiths Convention in Coventry, England. I took several guns with me and passed them out as mementos. The locksmiths there were most appreciative. An official of Scotland Yard was in attendance, and when I gave him the wire gun he expressed alarm that such a tool might get into the hands of the "other side" (i.e., criminals). Nonetheless, he wished me well and thanked me for the gun.

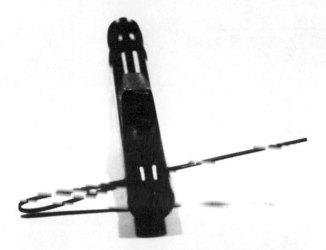

Detail of the Flare Gun pick's thumb trigger and doubled spring.

My local association, the Ontario Locksmiths, had their convention in the fall and I approached the H.P.C. reps (Hardware Products Corporation, a major supplier of locksmithing equipment) at their booth during the trade show. They were quite interested in the tool and took my name and a sample and promised to get back to me.

I heard nothing from them, but was later quite surprised to see an ad from H.P.C. showing my gun! It listed its features and included the closing notice: patent pending. I was nonplused and contacted them immediately. I spoke with their president, who remembered me from the show. He said he had lost my address and that I would be entitled to royalties based on sales of the Spring Pick Gun. I was mollified by this offer, but the story does demonstrate that the road to locksmith tool design and merchandising is a rocky one. If H.P.C. had wanted to, they could have cut me off completely. If nothing else, a confidential disclosure statement should have been signed and patent protection for the design secured. Let this experience be a lesson to all would-be inventors out there!

A

B

These wound-spring wire picks impart a snap action while picking—in effect, miniature pick guns. The A pick is for regular locks and the B pick is for double-sided pin-tumbler locks. The C tool is a wire tension wrench for a delicate touch. These may be homemade or purchased through KENCO or A-1.

C

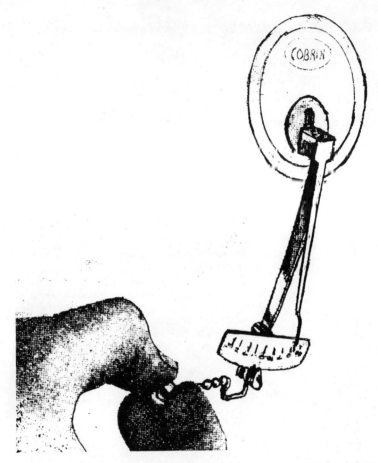

One of the big secrets of lock picking is the correct use of the tension wrench. Most beginners overdo the turning pressure. Delicacy of touch is achieved by calibrating the pressure with a torque wrench (shown here) in conjunction with the pick gun. A journal should be kept listing the successful attempts and torques used.

A modified Correx gram/pond, centi-newton tension meter used by Khris Balingit. It has a maximum-hold indicator and is used just like a normal tension wrench.

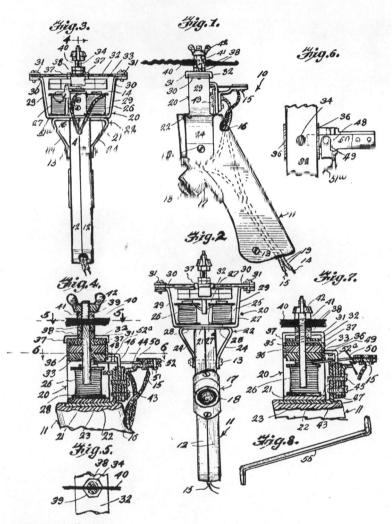

The Miskill patent.

Chapter Six

The Miskill Patent

UNITED STATES PATENT OFFICE

WILLIAM J. MISKILL, CHATTANOOGA, TENNESSEE

POWER-ACTUATED LOCK PICK

2,565,254. Specification of Letters Patent. Patented Aug. 21, 1951.
Application filed April 16, 1948. Serial No. 21,436.

This invention relates to an improved lock-picking machine for imparting a vibratory motion to a lock-picking blade and more particularly has reference to an electrically actuated mechanism for imparting a vibratory motion to the blade support.

Another object of the invention is to provide a machine of the aforedescribed character of extremely simple construction and wherein through the making and breaking of an electric circuit automatically accomplished in the operation of the machine, the constant vibratory motion of the lock-pick blade will be accomplished without the operator being required to execute any manual operation so that the implement, which is manually supported, can be accurately held and guided by the operator for accomplishing the lock-picking operation.

Still a further object of the invention is to provide a device for accomplishing the aforedescribed result, which is of extremely simple construction, capable of being economically manufactured and sold, and which will be very efficient and durable for its intended purpose.

Another object of the invention is to provide an implement whereby a lock-picking operation can be accomplished much more rapidly and with considerably less manual effort than is required in employing manually actuated lock-picking devices.

Various other objects and advantages of the invention will hereinafter become more fully apparent from the following description of the drawing, illustrating a presently preferred embodiment thereof, and wherein:

Figure 1 is a side elevational view of the assembled machine;

Figure 2 is a front elevational view thereof looking from left to right of Figure 1;

Figure 3 is a rear elevational view of the machine looking from right to left of Figure 1;

Figure 4 is a longitudinal sectional view, partly in side elevation taking substantially along a plane as indicated by the line 4—4 of Figure 3;

Figures 5 and 6 are horizontal cross sectional views taken substantially along planes as indicated by the lines 5—5 and 6—6, respectively, of Figure 4;

Figure 7 is a view similar to Figure 4 but showing the parts in a circuit-interrupting position, and

Figure 8 is a perspective view of a tool for use with the lock-picking blade.

Referring more specifically to the drawing, the novel lock-picking machine in its entirety and which is designated generally 10 includes a housing, designated generally 11 in the shape of a pistol grip and which is preferably formed of corresponding sections 12 detachably connected by fastenings 13. The housing 11 has two electrical conductors 14 and 15 extending therethrough from the lower end of said housing or grip 11 to adjacent the upper end thereof. Said conductors 14 and 15 project from the back edge of the housing 11 adjacent its upper end and through an opening 16 thereof, adjacent the upper end of said housing. A conventional electric switch, designated generally 17 is attached to the opposite, front edge of the housing or grip 11 and the conductor 15 is provided with spaced portions which are connected to the two contacts, not shown, of the switch 17 and whereby a gap is normally formed between said portions of the conductor 15 and which is adapted to be electrically bridged by pressing inwardly on the plunger or button 18 of the switch 17, all in a conventional manner. The conductors 14 and 15 are each enclosed in a tubing or casing 19 of a suitable insulating material, except portions of the conductor 15 which are connected to the switch 17 and the exposed ends of the conductors, as will hereinafter become apparent.

A yoke-shaped supporting frame 20 has a substantially flat intermediate portion 21 which is mounted on the upper end of the grip or housing 11 and transversely thereof. A bracket 22 has an intermediate portion suitably secured, as by welding, now shown, to the underside of the intermediate frame part 21 and which is disposed in a recess 23 at the upper end of the housing 11. The bracket 22 is provided with downwardly and inwardly curved free ends 24 having terminal portions which are apertured and which bear against corresponding portions of opposite sides of the housing 11 and through which the uppermost fastening 13 extends. Said fastening 13 comprises a headed bolt and nut.

A solenoid, designated generally 25, includes two corresponding units 26 and 27 which are suitably secured to the upper side of the intermediate portion 21 of the frame

20 and the coiled wires of which are connected by a conductor wire 27a, as seen in Figure 2. Solenoid units 26 and
27 are electrically insulated from the frame 20 by in-
sulators 28.

The frame 20 is provided with upwardly diverging arms
29 that rise from the ends of the intermediate portion 21,
outwardly of the solenoid 25, each of which arms terminates in an outturned terminal portion 30, which carries a
clamp 31. A normally flat spring 32, preferably formed of
two or more elongated resilient leaves, as best seen in Figures 4 and 7, is disposed above the solenoid 25 and with
the ends of the spring 32 secured to the terminals 30 by the
clamps 31.

An armature 33, illustrated as comprising two metallic
bars, has a rod 34 extending through the central portion
thereof and which is preferably fixed therein. The rod 34
also extends through an intermediate portion of the spring
32. A metal strip 35, through which the rod 34 extends, is
interposed between the armature 33 and spring 32 and has
downturned terminal portions 36 which engage opposite
sides of the armature 33 and upturned lugs or terminal portions 37 which engage the side edges of the spring 32 to
prevent the armature and rod 34 from turning relatively to
said spring. Accordingly, the armature 33 is disposed beneath and substantially in alignment and the spring 32
and with the solenoid 25. The upper end of the rod 34 is
threaded to receive two clamping nuts 38 by means of
which the armature is clamped to the spring 32 and above
said nuts 38, the rod 34 is longitudinally slotted as seen at
39 to detachably and adjustably receive the shank portion
of a lock-picking blade 40. A nut 41 engages the threaded
rod portion above the blade 40 for clamping the blade between said nut and the uppermost locking nut 38, and a
locking wing nut 42 engages the upper threaded end of the
rod 34 to retain the clamping nut 41 in adjusted position.

The bracket 22 is provided with an upstanding extension 43 which rises from the side edge thereof and which
extends outwardly from the housing 11 adjacent its outer

or rear edge, as best seen in Figures 1, 4, and 7. The supporting arm 43 supports an angular bracket 44, one leg of
which is connected to the outer side of said arm 43 by fastenings 45. Interposed between the arm 43 and the adjacent portion of the bracket 44 is a standard 46 through
which the fastenings 45 loosely extend and a strip of in
sulating material 47 is disposed on either side of the standard 46 for insulating said standard from the arm 43 and
bracket 44, as clearly illustrated in Figures 1 and 7. The
standard 46 is provided with an inturned upper end 48 carrying on its underside an electrical contact 49. A leaf
spring 50 is anchored by fastenings 51 and a retaining plate
52 to the upper side of the other end of the bracket 44 and
extends inwardly therefrom and has its free end disposed
beneath and in engagement with the underside of the
armature 33. The leaf spring 50, which is formed of a con-
ducting material, is provided with a contact 52a on the
upper side thereof and which is disposed to normally engage the contact 49.

As best seen in Figure 3, a conductor wire 51a connects
the coil of the solenoid unit 27 to a laterally extending portion of the standard 46 and as clearly illustrated in Figures
1 and 4, the end of the electrical conductor 15 which extends from the opening 16 is connected to one of the fastenings 51 thereby forming an electrical connection with
the contact 52a through the resilient conductor strip 50.
The corresponding end of the conductor wire 14 is connected to the coil of the solenoid unit 26.

The opposite ends of the conductors 14 and 15 are
adapted to be connected to any suitable source of electrical
current, not shown, preferably with a transformer interposed between the machine 10 and current source.

From the foregoing it will be readily apparent that the
circuit to the solenoid 25 will normally be interrupted by
the switch 17. The grip-shaped housing 11 can be grasped
in either hand and by applying one finger to the switch
plunger 18, said plunger can be pressed inwardly for bridging the gap between the conductor portions 15 for closing

the electric circuit to the solenoid 25, assuming that the conductors 14 and 15 are connected to a source of electric current. When this occurs, the solenoid 25 will be energized and magnetized for attracting the armature 33 downwardly. As the armature 33 is drawn downwardly, the spring 32 will be flexed downwardly and at the same time the resilient conductor strip 50 will also be caused to flex downwardly at its inner or forward end by its engagement with the armature 33. Accordingly, as the armature approaches the solenoid the resilient conductor strip 50 will draw the switch contact 52a out of engagement with the contact 49, thereby interrupting the electric circuit at the switch 49, 52a for de-energizing and demagnetizing the solenoid 25 so that the spring 32 will return the solenoid 33 from its position of Figure 7 back to its position of Figures 2, 3, and 4. As the solenoid 25 is thus moved upwardly, the resilient strip 50 will return to its position of Figure 4 thereby returning the contact 52a into engagement with the contact 49 for again energizing and magnetizing the solenoid 25 for repeating the operation just described. It will thus be readily apparent that the solenoid 25 will be alternately magnetized and in combination with the spring 32 will thereby impart a vibratory motion to the lock-pick blade 40 which is supported by said spring. Accordingly, so long as the plunger 18 is held depressed, the lock-pick blade 40 will be vibrated in a vertical plane to enable the proper impact to be imparted to the tumbler of a lock for accomplishing the lock-picking operation.

Figure 8 illustrates a tension implement 55, which is adapted to be disposed in the keyway of a lock to be picked beneath the blade 40 and for holding the lock-pick blade in the upper part of the keyway and in a position for impact engagement with the lock tumblers.

Various modifications and changes are contemplated and may obviously be resorted to, without departing from the spirit or scope of the invention as hereinafter defined by the appended claim:

I claim as my invention:

1. An electric lock-picking machine comprising a supporting structure adapted to be manually engaged and supported, a solenoid supported thereby and adapted to be connected to a source of electric current, an armature for said solenoid, a resilient support connected to said supporting structure for supporting said armature in spaced relationship to the solenoid, means connected to said resilient support for supporting a lock-pick blade thereabove and for movement therewith, an electric switch interposed in the electric circuit of the solenoid and including a fixed contact and a resilient contact, and said resilient contact having a portion disposed beneath and in engagement with the armature whereby when the solenoid is energized and magnetized for attracting the armature, said resilient contact will be moved by the armature to a circuit interrupting position for de-energizing the solenoid, and said resilient support reacting to move the armature away from the solenoid when the solenoid is demagnetized.

2. An electric lock pick as in claim 1, said supporting structure including a yoke-shaped frame in which said solenoid is fixedly disposed, said frame having upstanding side members, clamping means on the upper ends of said side members for detachably engaging and clamping the ends of the resilient support to the frame and for positioning the resilient support above the solenoid.

3. An electric lock-picking machine comprising a manually supported supporting structure, a solenoid fixedly supported thereby, a spring bridging a portion of said supporting structure, an armature supported by said spring in spaced relationship to the supporting structure, means mounted by said spring for adjustably and detachably mounting a lock-picking blade, said solenoid being electrically energized for attracting the armature and flexing said spring, a switch interposed in the electric circuit to the solenoid including a movable contact, and a resilient member normally supporting the movable contact in a circuit closing position and disposed to be engaged and moved by the armature to move the movable contact to a

circuit interrupting position for interrupting the circuit when the armature is drawn toward the solenoid, said spring reacting to move the armature away from the solenoid when the latter is de-energized for closing the switch and re-energizing the solenoid.

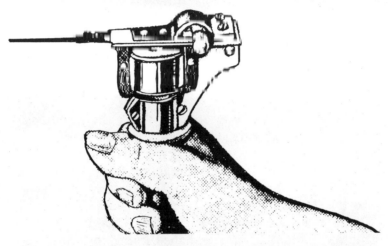

A modified Dremel jigsaw with a pick needle attached to its vibratory mechanism. It is strikingly similar in concept and execution to the Miskill patent, which itself is based on the doorbell-clapper unit.

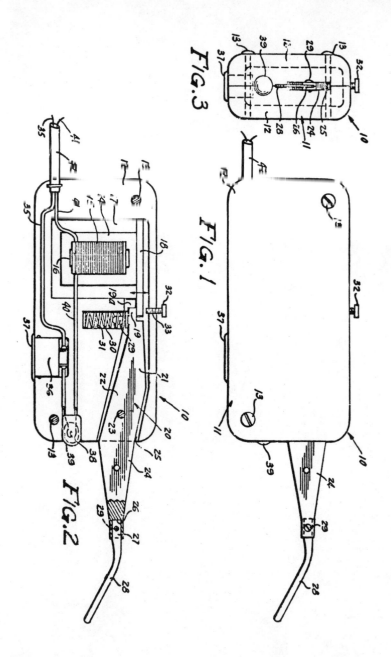

The Moore patent.

Chapter Seven

The Moore Patent

UNITED STATES PATENT OFFICE

LLOYD L. MOORE, PORTLAND, OREGON

VIBRATORY LOCK PICK

3,264,908. Specification of Letters Patent. Patented August 9, 1966.

Application filed August 24, 1964. Serial No. 391523.

This invention relates to a lock pick, and more particularly to an electrically actuated lock pick including a vibratory needle, which is adapted to be inserted into the key opening of pin-tumbler or wafer locks to facilitate the work of a locksmith in the unlocking of such locks.

A primary object of this invention is the provision of an improved lock pick of this character having means whereby upon connecting the device to a source of alternating current, the pick will be automatically vibrated or oscillated at a relatively high rate of speed in order to facilitate the alignment of the pin tumblers or wafers, so that the lock may be readily opened by means of a conventional turning wrench.

An additional object of the invention is the provision of such a device which may be readily adapted for insertion into a six-volt converter, which in turn is connected to a portable battery so that the device may be used in any location.

A further object of the invention is the provision of such a device which is provided with a body in the form of a compact handle, the latter being provided with an external telltale light and an actuating switch in a position readily accessible to the operator.

A still further object of the invention is the provision of a device of this character that is provided internally with an electromagnetic coil, which, when connected to alternating current, will impart oscillatory vibration to a bar, which will in turn impart such vibration to a lever, at the end of which is mounted the needle comprising the lock pick per se.

A still further object of the invention is the provision of a device of this character that is sturdy and durable in construction, relatively compact and easy to transport and manipulate, reliable and efficient in operation, simple and inexpensive to manufacture, and simple and efficient in use and operation.

Still other objects will in part be obvious and in part be pointed out as the description of the invention proceeds, and disclosed in the accompanying drawing wherein there is shown a preferred embodiment of this inventive concept.

In the drawing:

FIGURE 1 is a side elevational view of the lock pick of the instant invention.

FIGURE 2 is a longitudinal sectional view taken substantially through the center line thereof; and

FIGURE 3 is an end elevational view of the devices of

FIGURES 1 and 2 as viewed from the right.

Similar reference characters refer to similar parts throughout the several views of the drawing.

Having reference now to the drawings in detail, there is generally indicated at 10 an electric lock pick constructed in accordance with the instant invention which includes a body 11 comprised of two separable halves 12, which are secured together as by means of screws or bolts 13. A centrally positioned cavity in the center of the body contains a wire wound coil 15 surrounding a laminated core 16, adjacent which is a U shaped magnet 17, having its poles projecting upwardly. The magnet ends have positioned thereacross a metallic bar 18, one end of which extends beyond one leg of the magnet into an adjacent cavity 19a, and abuts the underside of a horizontal arm 19 comprising a part of a lever 20. The lever includes an upwardly and rearwardly inclined portion 21 and a central portion 22, through the midpoint of which a pivot 23 extends. The lever also includes an outwardly extending tapered portion 24, which projects through a narrow slotted opening 25 in the front of the casing and terminates in a socket 26. The socket contained in the shank 27 of a lock-pick needle 28, which is held in position in the socket by means of a set screw 29. The needle 28 is adapted for insertion in the key opening of a pin-tumbler lock, for a purpose to be more fully described hereinafter.

A depending lug 29 adjacent arm 19 engages one end of a coil spring 30, which is set in a socket 31, and which serves normally to bias the upper portion of horizontal arm 19 into engagement with the lower side of the extending end of bar 18.

A set screw 32 extends through a threaded opening 33 in the top wall of the casing and may be adjusted to limit the range of the oscillatory vibration imparted to the bar, and hence the pivotal oscillation of the lever 20 and its associated needle 23.

Current is supplied to coil 15 through a first wire 35, which extends through a switch 36 operated by a button or slide 37 located exteriorly of the casing, and thence through the filament 38 of a telltale or indicator bulb 39. From the other end of the filament 38 a wire 40 leads directly to the coil 15, from which a wire 41 returns to a common wire conduit 42. The conduit 42 terminates in a conventional electric plug, which may be inserted in any wall outlet for a source of alternating current Alternatively, the plug may be connected to an inverter and employed in conjunction with a battery supplying direct current to the inverter

In the use and operation of the device, the needle or pick is inserted in the key opening of a tumbler lock, the switch 37 moved to circuit-closing position, after connection of the conduit 42 to a suitable source of alternating current, and the operation of the device occasioned by the vibration of the bar 18 and the consequent oscillatory pivotal vibration of the lever 20 agitates the pin tumblers into alignment so that the lock may be turned or opened after aligning the tumblers by means of an ordinary or conventional locksmith's turning wrench.

Obviously, the use of such a device facilitates and expedites the work of a locksmith, since the rapid vibratory movement has the effect of aligning the pin tumblers with extreme rapidity and simplicity, and requires no particular skill in its use and operation.

From the foregoing it will now be seen that there is herein provided an improved lock pick that accomplishes all of the objects of this invention, and others, including many advantages of great practical utility and commercial importance.

As many embodiments may be made of this invention concept, and as many modifications may be made in the embodiment hereinbefore shown and described, it is to be understood that all matter herein is to be interpreted merely as illustrative, and not in a limiting sense.

I claim:

1. A lock pick comprising, in combination, a body forming a handle, a laminated core surrounded by a coil in said

body, a magnet adjacent said coil and selectively energizable thereby, an elongated bar mounted for oscillating movement in said body adjacent said magnet, an electric circuit connected to said coil, means for connecting said circuit to a source of alternating current to impart oscillating vibration to said bar, a lever pivoted in said body having one end in contact with said bar for oscillating vibration thereby and its other end extending outwardly through an opening in said body, and a needle adapted to be inserted into the key opening of a tumbler lock for vibrating the tumblers thereof fitted to said other end.

2. The structure of claim 1 wherein said circuit includes an electric switch, and means exteriorly of said body for closing and opening said switch.

3. The structure of claim 2 wherein said circuit includes an indicator light visible from the exterior of said casing, and illuminated when said circuit is closed by said switch.

4. The structure of claim 1 wherein a compression spring in said body engages said lever to bias said one end into continuous contact with said bar.

5. The structure of claim 4 wherein said lever includes a central portion through which the pivot extends, an upwardly extending portion terminating in a horizontal arm abutting the underside of said bar, an adjacent vertical lug engaging the end of said coil spring, and a downwardly extending tapered portion extending outwardly through said opening and having a socket at its outer end, said needle sitting in said socket, and a set screw for retaining said needle in said socket.

6. The structure of claim 1 wherein a set screw is threaded through the wall of said body adjacent one end of said bar for regulating the oscillation thereof.

Battery-powered scissors form the basis for this electrical pick gun made by the author. Note the similarities to the Moore patent and its advantage of being portable. My sister, when just a schoolgirl, picked her first lock with this device with no previous lock-pick training.

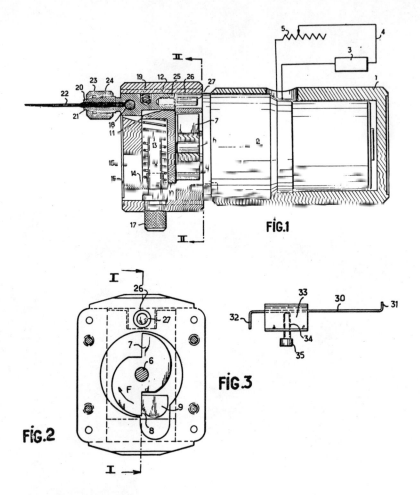

FIG.1

FIG.2

FIG.3

The Crasnianski patent.

Chapter Eight

The Crasnianski Patent

UNITED STATES PATENT OFFICE

SERGE CRASNIANSKI, GRENOBLE, FRANCE

APPARATUS FOR PICKING
PIN-TUMBLER CYLINDER LOCKS

4,156,375. Specification of Letters Patent. Patented May 29, 1979.

Application Filed September 20, 1977. Application No. 835,149.

This invention concerns a method of picking a cylinder lock of the pin-tumbler type and a lock-pick apparatus embodying the method, such as are useful for opening a lock of that type when the key has been lost and cannot be replaced.

In such cylinder locks, the closure is secured in the locked condition by a plurality of spring-loaded counter-pins in the stator of the lock extending into the bores into which they respectively press the pin tumblers of the cylindrical rotor of the lock. The pin tumblers and counter-pins are so made that the projections and recesses on the key bit shift the tumblers, and with them the counter-pins, when the key is inserted, to the correct extend against the respective springs, so that the separation surface between pin tumbler and counter-pin brought exactly in alignment with the boundary between rotor and stator (cylinder and casing respectively). The cylinder can then be rotated so as to open the lock.

If the key to such a lock is lost or misplaced, it is possible only with the greatest difficulty to obtain by any other means the simultaneous precise shift of the individual pin tumblers and counter-pins, against the force of the springs, that will enable the lock to be opened.

It is known how to pick such a lock by means of a pistol-grip device carrying a pick needle in an operative position suitable for feeling out the tumblers and equipped with a trigger-operated mechanism for setting the needle into vibrations, in order to apply the vibrations to the tumblers and to the counter-pins and thereby to press the latter back into the stator. During that operation, a rotary force is applied to the cylinder by means of a bent tool, so that the cylinder will turn as soon as the counter-pins have been forced back into the casing by acting on the tumblers. The ends of the auxiliary tool for exerting a rotary force on the cylinder are made in various ways and a set of such tools can be provided for opening locks of a variety of individual types. The operator, normally an experienced locksmith, inserts one end, namely a bent-over portion of the tool, into the keyway of the lock and presses on the other end to apply a rotary force to the cylinder. While rotary force is applied in this way, the locksmith inserts the needle of the pistol-grip tool into the keyway and seeks to determine the position of the tumblers and the exact place and position in which the needle can best be effective in order to align the tumblers in accordance with the unlocking combination. After he has performed this exploring function by feeling out the lock, he presses on the trigger, in order to vibrate the needle with a sudden movement.

It has been found in practice that opening a lock with such a gun tool and an auxiliary tool requires an inordinately large amount of time. It generally takes a half hour before an experienced locksmith can open a cylinder lock with these tools. The reason for the difficulty is that both of the hands of the locksmith are needed for this method of operation, one hand for holding the auxiliary tool and the other one for the opening instrument. Furthermore, the hand of the locksmith with which he holds the opening instrument must also at the same time actuate the trigger for the vibratory drive. These different manipulations, on the one hand the necessary fingertip feeling to explore the tumblers and on the other hand the force for pulling the trigger to release the vibratory movement, produce difficulties. Finally, the force that it is necessary to expend in order to apply force to the mechanism through the trigger until the release point of the mechanism is reached often results in loss of the exact position of the needle that has been laboriously established beforehand.

U.S. Pat. No. 3,264,908 disclosed a device, likewise in gun form, having a pick needle for insertion in the keyway of the lock for movement of the tumblers and counterpins, in which a weight is mounted so that it may swing about an axis, equipped to be excited into vibration by means of an electromagnet and a spring. The electromagnet is in this case connected to an alternating current supply, so that the weight and the needle execute sinusoidal vibrations.

With the device just described, the lock-picking operation is indeed simplified, because the operator no longer needs to apply force to generate the vibratory movement of the pick needle and can therefore insert and place the gun-like tool more accurately, but a rapid alignment of the tumblers in the cylinder of the lock is still not possible, even with this device.

It is an object of the present invention to provide a method and apparatus for picking pin-tumbler cylinder locks in which the above-described disadvantages are overcome and which will make possible the opening of the lock by a sudden movement. It is an object of the invention to enable such opening of locks in less than a minute, relieving the operator of the device entirely from all operations requiring the application of force, for example for pressing a trigger, so that the operator can direct all his skill to finding a favorable position for the pick needle in the lock. It is also an object of the invention to provide an auxiliary tool that will enable him to hold the pick device with both hands.

Briefly, the lock-pick tool has a pick needle arranged to be struck one or more times towards the counter-pins with so much energy that tumbler and counter-pin will separate as the counter-pin is thrown back into the locked casing (stator). In the method according to the invention, contrary to operations according to the disclosure of the above-mentioned U.S. patent, a shock or power pulse is applied to each individual tumbler, which shock or pulse is of such magnitude in energy that on the basis of the laws of conservation of momentum and of energy, the counter-pin abutting the end of the tumbler opposite to the end that receives the impact of the stroke separates from the tumbler and is driven back into the casing (stator) against its loading spring.

The method according to the invention can be performed particularly well with a lock-pick device according to the invention in which a pick needle is fastened to a massive member in a hand-grip tool, for pressing back and adjusting the pin tumblers and counterpins, but in which, in contrast to the device described in the above-mentioned patent, a hammer is provided for applying an impact stroke on the tumblers through the pick needle, the hammer being thrown against the massive element carrying the pick needle in each stroke by an energy storage device charged by an electric motor drive.

In order to perform the movements for generating a stroke and applying its impact on the pick needle, a preferred form of the invention utilizes a drive using a rotary cam with an effectively linear lifting or retracting characteristic and sudden return stroke for first retracting the hammer from the massive member against a spring operating as an energy storage device and then releasing the spring to drive the hammer suddenly. The cam drive is in this case driven by an electric motor through a reduction gear in such a way that the hammer delivers individual impacts to the massive member at a sufficient spacing in time to allow transient oscillations following the stroke to die down between strokes. Quick opening of a cylinder lock is made possible in this way, because even after a few strokes, the individual counter-pins are so driven back that rotation of the cylinder in the lock casing is possible.

Since an electric motor drive is provided, the operator does not need to apply any substantial force in order to manipulate the device or to produce the oscillations of the pick needle.

By a further development of the invention, means are provided for adjusting the energy of each impact, the stroke length, and the repetition rate of the impacts. The energy of the impact can be adjusted by variation of the bias of the spring, against which the hammer is moved by the cam drive. The stroke length can be determined by limiting the movement range of the weight (massive member) by means of a simple adjustment pin, and the repetition rate of the strokes can be determined by adjustment of the rate of rotation of the electric motor drive, which is most simply done by means of a rheostat in the current supply circuit of the drive. Since in this mode of operation it is not necessary to feel out the position of the individual tumblers, it is also not necessary to provide the pick needle in a bent shape. It is sufficient, rather, to provide in a simple cylindrical or parallel-piped rod shape, which is very easy to handle and manipulate.

The invention is further described by way of illustrative

example with reference to the annexed drawings, in which:

FIG. 1 is a longitudinal section passing through the central axis of the casing of a lock pick according to the invention;

FIG. 2 is a section to the line II-II of FIG. 1; and

FIG. 3 is a top view of an auxiliary tool carrying out the method of the invention.

As shown in FIG. 1, an electric motor drive including reduction gearing, collectively designated 2, is housed in a casing 1 consisting of two pieces held together with flanges. The drive is powered by a battery 3 to which it is connected by means of wire 4 and an interposed rheostat 5, the battery and rheostat having their own common housing.

At the free end of the shaft 6 of the reduction gear drive 2, a cam 7 is keyed to the shaft. The cam has two linear lifting curves (FIG. 2) (i.e. linear relation between radius and angle), each leading to a sudden step 8. The cam operates on a cam follower 9 that is part of a hammer 10, the end 11 of which strikes against a massive member 12 that operates as a weight set in motion by the stroke of the hammer. A restoring spring 13 bears at one end against the inner surface of the end 11 of the hammer 10 and at the other end against a nut 14 that has a guiding extension 15 that slides in a guideway 15a that is a cavity in the casing of the device. The nut 14 can be shifted axially by turning of a screw 16 by means of the knurled knob 17 in order to change the bias of the spring 13.

The massive member 12 can pivot on an axle rod 18 mounted in the casing. The swinging stroke of the member 12 is executed against the force of a spring 19 that presses the member 12 against the hammer 10, so that the massive lever 12 moves clockwise about the axle 18 by a certain amount when the hammer 10 is moved downwards.

The free end 20 of the massive lever 12 operates externally. It has a chuck 21 in which a pick needle 22 is held by means of a clamping nut 23 that is screwed onto the external threads 24 of the chuck. At the end 25 of the massive lever 12 on the opposite side of the axle 18 from the end 20 there is provided a cavity 26 in which the pin 27 set in the end of the lever 12 can move freely. By axial adjustment of the position of the pin 27, the stroke length of the pivoting movement of the lever 12 can be adjusted

FIG. 3 shows an auxiliary tool consisting of a strip 30, preferably made of metal, the ends of which are bent over in opposite directions. On the strip itself a counterweight 33 can be shifted along its mid-portion. This counterweight 33 has a threaded bore 34 for seating a set screw 35 for the purpose of fixing the position of the counterweight 33 on the strip 30.

To operate with the lock pick according to the invention, the user holds the lock pick by the casing 1. The motor 2 turns the cam that at regular intervals releases the driving pin 9 of the hammer 10 in such a way that the end 11 of the hammer 10 suddenly strikes the massive lever 12 as a hammer 10 is driven by the spring 16 that serves as the energy storage device of the system. The massive lever thus provides the stroke by a counterclockwise rotary movement about the axis 18 to the pick needle 22, the amplitude of the stroke being limited by the abutment of the pin 27 against the wall of the casing cavity 26.

By more or less rotation of the holding screw knob 17 and corresponding axial shift of the nut 14, the operator can change the degree of bias of the spring 16 and thereby the force with which the hammer 10 strikes the massive lever 12.

By variation of the resistance in the current supply circuit 4 of the electric motor by means of the rheostat 5, the rotation speed of the drive motor 2 and hence that of the cam 7 can be changed. In that way the repetition rate of the strokes of the hammer 10 on the massive lever 12 and hence the impact frequency of the needle 22 can be varied.

When the bent-over end 31 of the strip 30 is inserted in a lock, the counterweight 33 on the strip 30 causes a torque to be exerted on the cylinder on the lock without requiring the operator to hold the auxiliary tool in his hand. By shifting the counterweight along the strip 30, the torque applied can be adjusted, so that between the adjustment of the motor-driven pick and the adjustment of the torque of the auxiliary tool, it is possible to utilize the equipment and method of the present invention successfully on a wide variety of cylinder locks.

Although the invention has been described with reference to a particular illustrative embodiment, it will be understood that variations are possible within the inventive concept.

I claim:

1. A dynamic lock pick, for picking a cylinder lock having a plurality of pin tumblers in the cylinder resting in the locked condition respectively against spring-loaded counter-pins housed in a stator, an end of each of the pin tumblers being accessible in a keyway, said pick comprising:

    a. positioning; casing of a size and shape suitable for manual positioning;

    b. a pick needle 22 insertable in the keyway of a cylinder lock and mounted on a massive member located mainly within said casing and movable over a limited range of positions relative to said casing in a direction corresponding to movement of said pick needle transversely in said keyway;

    c. means 27 for adjusting the range of movement of said massive member 12 in said casing and thereby adjusting the stroke length of said pick needle;

    d. A hammer 11 movable mounted in said casing for hitting said massive member 12 carrying said pick needle so as to transmit shock to said pin tumblers when said pick needle is in the keyway of a cylinder lock;

    e. a mechanical energy-storage member 13 in said casing and bearing against said hammer;

    f. an electric motor drive 2 for alternately storing energy in said energy-storage member 13 by moving said hammer against said energy-storage member and releasing said hammer and energy-storage member suddenly to cause said hammer 11 to be thrown against said massive element 12 carrying said pick needle 22; and

g. a restoring spring 19 for urging said massive member 12 in a direction towards such hammer for returning said massive element to the position of the beginning of a stroke.

2. A lock pick as defined in claim 1, in which said energy-storage member in a spring 13 in said casing and in which said electric motor drive 2 includes a rotary cam 7 for alternately moving said hammer 11 against the force of said spring 13 and releasing said hammer and said spring.

3. A lock pick as defined in claim 2, comprising also means 14, 16, 17 for adjusting the bias force of said spring 13 exerted against said hammer 11.

4. A lock pick as defined in claim 3, in which said adjusting means 14, 16 includes a screw having a knurled head accessible from the outside of said casing.

5. A lock pick as defined in claim 2, in which said movement range adjusting means includes an adjustable pin 27 movable in a cavity 26 of said casing, said adjustable pin 27 being so mounted adjustably on said massive member 12 that at the extremes of the stroke length set by its adjustment, its end lies against an edge of said opening 26.

6. A lock pick as defined in claim 1, comprising also means for adjusting the repetition rate of hammer strokes produced by said electric motor drive 2 by adjusting the supply of power to the electric motor of said electric motor drive.

7. A lock pick as defined in claim 6, in which said repetition rate adjusting means is a stepless adjusting means.

8. A lock pick as defined in claim 7, in which said stepless adjusting means is a rheostat 5.

9. An auxiliary tool for a trip hammered vibrating lock pick comprising a metal strip 30 bent over at right angles at both ends 31, 32 in respectively opposite directions and

an adjustable weight 3 slidably mounted on the mid-portion of said strip between its bent ends and having means 34, 35 for fixing it at a selected position on said strip.

10. An auxiliary tool for a lock pick as defined in claim 9, in which said fixing means for said adjustable weight include a said screw 35 for releasably fixing said weight longitudinally of said mid portion of said strip.

Chapter Nine

Agency Lock-Opening Device

AGENCY LOCK-OPENING DEVICE
OPERATING INSTRUCTIONS

_____

List of Items

1 – Lock Opening Device
1 – Attachment #1
1 – Attachment #2
1 – Attachment #3
1 – Attachment #4
5 – Picks
1 – Universal Charger
1 – External Battery Cable
1 – Line Plug Adaptor
2 – Allen Wrenches
1 – Instruction Booklet
1 – Leather Carrying Case

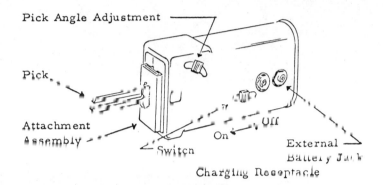

Pick Angle Adjustment

Pick

Attachment
Assembly

Switch

On   Off

External
Battery Jack

Charging Receptacle

GENERAL VIEW OF DEVICE

FIG. 1

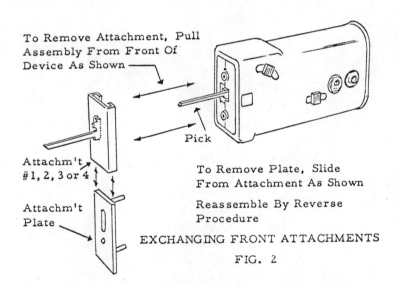

To Remove Attachment, Pull
Assembly From Front Of
Device As Shown

Pick

Attachm't
#1, 2, 3 or 4

Attachm't
Plate

To Remove Plate, Slide
From Attachment As Shown

Reassemble By Reverse
Procedure

EXCHANGING FRONT ATTACHMENTS

FIG. 2

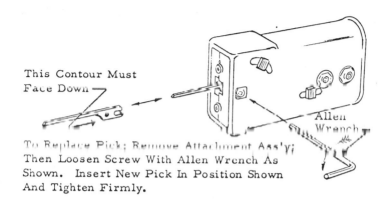

This Contour Must
Face Down

Allen
Wrench

To Replace Pick; Remove Attachment Ass'y;
Then Loosen Screw With Allen Wrench As
Shown. Insert New Pick In Position Shown
And Tighten Firmly.

PICK REPLACEMENT

FIG. 3

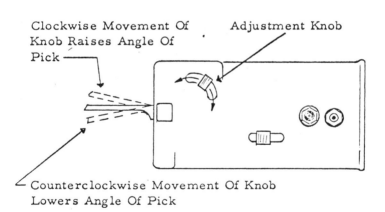

Clockwise Movement Of
Knob Raises Angle Of
Pick

Adjustment Knob

Counterclockwise Movement Of Knob
Lowers Angle Of Pick

PICK ANGLE ADJUSTMENT

FIG. 4

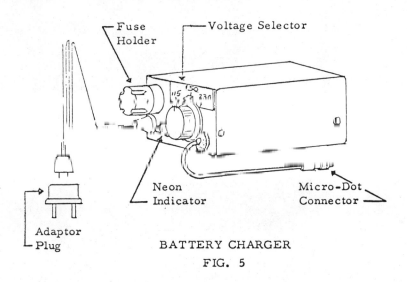

BATTERY CHARGER

FIG. 5

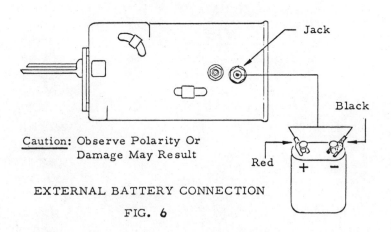

Caution: Observe Polarity Or
Damage May Result

EXTERNAL BATTERY CONNECTION

FIG. 6

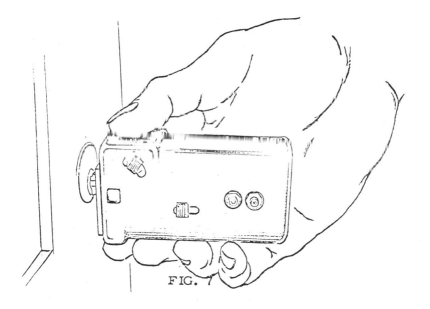

FIG. 7

General Description

The Lock-Opening Device is a self-powered electromechanical device designed to permit rapid opening of a specific group of pin-tumbler locks manufactured by Zeiss-Ikon, Yale, BKS, and others using similar style keyways (see Figs. 1 and 7). An opening is usually effected within 20 seconds.

Power is provided by two self-contained nickel-cadmium batteries, which permit twenty minutes or more of total operation without recharge. Recharging in one hour is possible by use of the universal charger provided, which operates on 90 to 250 volts of 50- or 60-cycle current.

The device is provided with four attachments that are readily replaceable and are designed to permit insertion into the greatest number of various keyways. These are numbered 1, 2, 3, and 4 and have been classified in the following manner. For the purpose of simplification, keyways were divided into four broad categories—left-hand, right-hand, curved and straight—thus making a total of four attachments of the following combinations:

#1: Right-Hand Curved
#2: Left-Hand Curved
#3: Right-Hand Straight
#4: Left-Hand Straight

These attachments are easily exchanged by following the instructions in Fig. 2. A leather key case is provided with two holders to carry the attachments.

Two lengths of picks are provided to permit the opening of either the five-pin or six-pin locks. The exchange or replacement of these is covered by Fig. 3.

Attachments

Four stainless-steel attachments are provided to permit insertion into various keyways and are marked by the numbers 1, 2, 3, and 4 stamped on the front of each attachment.

Reference is made to the following page showing enlarged views of typical keyways with the area occupied by the attachment (crosshatched area) and the pick (solid area) clearly indicated. The views shown are those seen when facing the front of the lock plug and typify right-handed and left-handed keyways of both the curved and straight types.

Attachment #1 is designed to be used on *right*-handed keyways of the curved type and as seen from the view shown consists of a *right* facing angular member, which enters the lower part of the keyway, and a *right* curved member, which enters the extreme top portion of the keyway. This places the pick in the best position for optimum results.

Attachment #2 is designed to be used on *left*-handed keyways of the curved type and consists of a *left* facing angular member which enters the lower part of the keyway and a *left* curved member which enters the very top of the keyway.

As shown in the enlarged views, Attachment #3 is for *right*-handed straight keyways and Attachment #4 is for *left*-handed straight keyways. These are very similar to #1 and #2 except that the member that enters the very top of the keyway is a straight section. Attachments #3 and #4 have been designed to hold the pick at an angle in the keyway to permit proper impact with the pins.

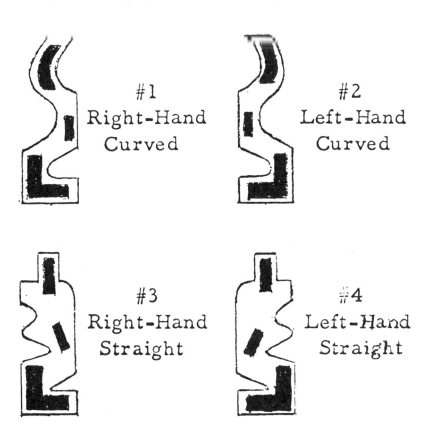

#1
Right-Hand
Curved

#2
Left-Hand
Curved

#3
Right-Hand
Straight

#4
Left-Hand
Straight

TYPICAL KEYWAYS

BKS   YALE   ZEISS-IKON   BKS   YALE   ZEISS-IKON

XN1   ZN1

N3

ABUS CISA   ABUS CISA

ATTACHMENT #1   ATTACHMENT #2

YALE

GA   GB   GC   GD

BKS

GE   GF   GG   GH

GK

NJK
82

ATTACHMENT #3   ATTACHMENT #3

BKS

| CMWS | GMWT | GMWW | GMWX |
| 1 | 1 | 1 | 1 |

| GMWY | GMVM | GYVV | GYVW |
| 1 | 1 | 1 | 1 |

ATTACHMENT #4

Operation
1) Select proper attachment and pick and install on device (Figs. 1 and 2).
2) Set pick-angle selector to center position of its adjustment (Fig. 4) and insert device into keyway.
3) Actuate slide switch to start mechanism and, while supporting device between thumb and fingers, allow device to seek a neutral position in keyway.
4) Apply a very light rotational force in the direction an opening is desired, momentarily releasing and reapplying this force each three to four strokes until an opening is effected. In the event an opening is not effected, alternate positions of the pick-angle selector should be tried along with slight lifting or lowering of the device while the mechanism is in operation.
Important: The lightest rotational force is the best assurance that an opening will be effected.

Battery Recharging
Rechargeable nickel-cadmium batteries are used to power the device and require recharging on a regular basis to insure proper operation. See Fig. 5. To recharge batteries:
1) Connect the universal charger to the device by means

of the connecting cable and microdot fitting provided.

2) Rotate the voltage-selector switch to the 230-volt position and insert the line plug into a wall outlet.

3) Rotate the selector switch counterclockwise until the neon indicator glows. This indicates the proper transformer tap has been selected for the line voltage provided.

Caution. Be certain to select the 230-volt tap before inserting plug, or the fuse will be blown. In the event the fuse has been blown, the neon indicator will not glow on any position of the selector switch and a new fuse must be installed.

The charging rate is approximately 1 ampere and is capable of recharging the batteries in one to two hours, but longer periods are permissible.

After charging at the 1-ampere rate, continued charging at a reduced rate is possible by rotating the selector switch to the next higher voltage position (called a *trickle charge*). This provides a charging rate of approximately .1 ampere and can be used to keep the batteries in top charge condition for extended periods of time.

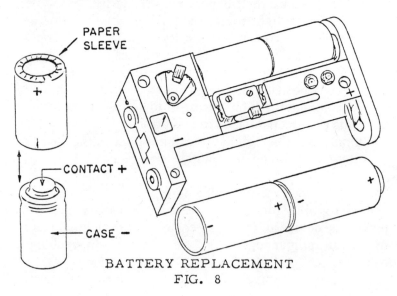

PAPER
SLEEVE

CONTACT +

CASE −

BATTERY REPLACEMENT
FIG. 8

Battery Replacement

The nickel-cadmium batteries used to power the Lock-Opening Device should never need replacing with normal use and regular charging; however, in the event replacement should become necessary, refer to Fig. 8. This view shows the device with the vinyl cover removed and the polarity marking engraved in the housing. The insulating sleeves shown must be used on the new batteries.

The vinyl cover is removed by first removing the pick-angle adjusting knob by using the small Allen wrench provided and then sliding the cover off the device. The batteries can now be readily removed from their mounting and new ones installed, being careful to observe the polarity markings and using the original insulating sleeves provided. The batteries originally supplied with the device are Sonotone S113 and are used quite extensively in electric shavers and electric toothbrushes and should be available at service centers in many countries.

The Agency Lock-Opening Device. The turning member is not fitted. (Photo courtesy of H.K. Melton.)

The Agency Lock-Opening Device with accompanying manual and
Buxton key wallets for spare parts. This device is unique in that the
tension-wrench equivalent is built-in so that locks may be opened with
one hand—just like in the movies.

The original Agency lock pick came in a clear Lucite case about the
size of a pocket novel. The picks were round needles of various shapes,
and a rheostat controlled the speed of impact. These devices appeared
to be based on a buzzer unit and were battery-operated, as I remember.
(Photo courtesy of H.K. Melton.)

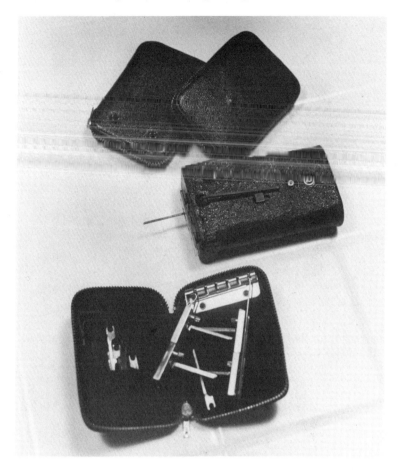

The Agency Lock-Opening Device with pick needles and keyway-suited turning wrenches. (Photo courtesy of H.K. Melton.)

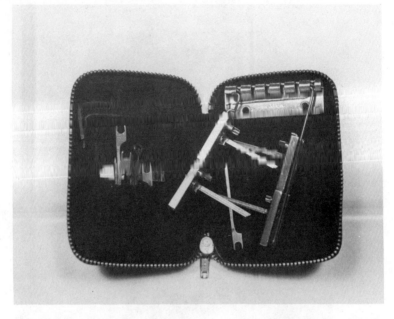

Close-up of turning wrenches and pick-needle wallet. (Photo courtesy of H.K. Melton.)

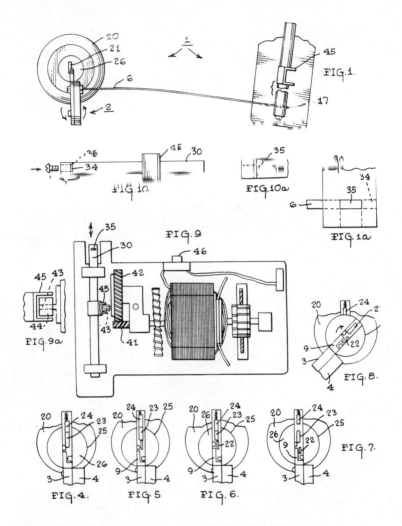

The Cooke patent. It is a truly revolutionary pick gun.

Chapter Ten

The Cooke Patent

UNITED STATES PATENT OFFICE

ROBERT G. COOKE, JR., AHOSKIE,
NORTH CAROLINA

SYSTEM AND APPARATUS FOR
OPENING CYLINDER LOCKS

4,606,204. Specification of Letters Patent. Patented Aug. 19, 1986.
Application filed December 27, 1983. Application No. 565,403.

Background of the Invention

This invention relates to a method of opening a wide variety of modern locks in common use and a lock-opening mechanism embodying the method. More specifically, this invention relates to a new and improved method and apparatus to facilitate the opening of a variety of security

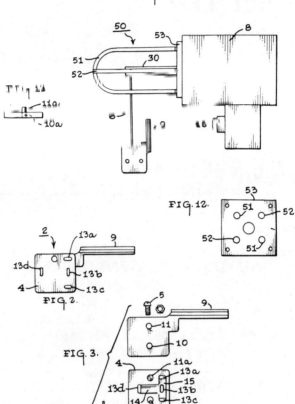

FIG. 11.

50 53 8
51 30
52
8
9
18

FIG. 12.
53
51 52
52 51

2
13a 9
13d
13b
4 13c
FIG. 2.

FIG. 3.
5
9
11
10
4 11a
13a
15
13d 13b
14 13c
16 10a 6

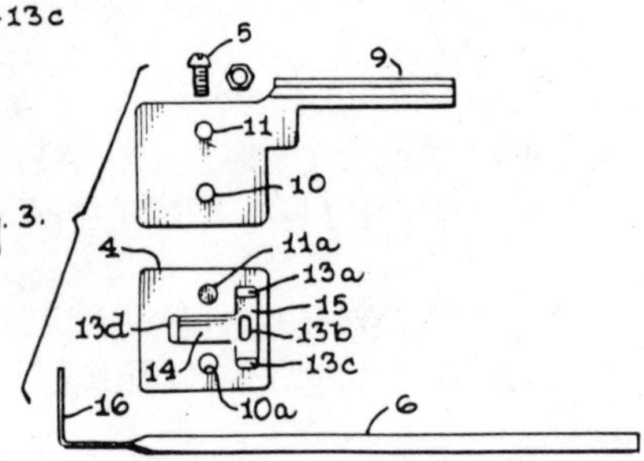

locks, including disc-tumbler, wafer-tumbler, and pin-tumbler cylinder type locks when the key has either been lost or misplaced.

While it is the endeavor of lock craftsmen to design pickproof locking devices, it is known among experts of the lock making industry that a key-operated lock mechanism is subject to picking. However, it is not a simple task for the lock artist to design and construct an in strument to pick a real security lock. As a result of exten sive laboratory research, many present day locks, while not pickproof, are pick resistant and will stubbornly resist attempts to pick them. Consequently, lock picking itself has demanded a great deal of expert knowledge, skill, and a considerable amount of study. Most typically, it is known how to pick pin-tumbler cylinder locks by means of a device carrying a pick-needle member with a trigger operated means for setting the needle, inserted into the keyway, into vibration in order to apply vibrations to the tumblers and counterpins. During this operation, a rotary force is applied to the lock cylinder. It has been found in practice that opening a lock with such a device requires skill and an inordinately large amount of time.

U.S. Pat. No. 4,156,375 to Crasnianski disclosed a lock-pick mechanism comprising a motor driven cam in order to impart a shock motion to the pick needle member, which is inserted into the lock keyway. The pick needle of the Crasnianski device is arranged on a member to be struck repeatedly by the end of a hammer to impart a shock or pulse to the pick needle. U.S. Pat. No. 3,264,908 to Moore also disclosed a vibratory lock device comprising an electromagnetic motor that imparts a vibratory motion to the pick needle so that the lock may be opened by means of a turning wrench. U.S. Pat. No. 2,565,254 to Mis-kill discloses a power-actuated lock pick that operates in a manner very similar to that disclosed in the Moore patent. The Miskill reference disclosed the use of continuous vi-brational motion, which is imparted to a lock-pick blade. Miskill further disclosed a tension member, which is adapted to be inserted into the keyway to a lock beneath the lock pick in order to hold the lock pick in the upper part of the keyway in a position for impact engagement with the lock tumbler pins.

Summary of the Invention

It is an object of this invention to provide an improved method and apparatus to be used by initiated lock craftsmen and law enforcement officials as an instrument for opening all standard makes of pin and wafer cylinder locks in a minimum of time. Many locks can be opened in a matter of seconds. It is also an object of the invention to provide a lock-opening mechanism that can be conveniently, economically, and rapidly assembled. Another object of this invention is to provide a mechanism for enabling the lockmaster and law enforcement officials to open high grade locks while requiring very little, if any, skill on the part of the operator.

Still another object of this invention is to provide an oscillating mechanism that operates to rotate lock cylinders back and forth repeatedly in a very rapid movement to facilitate their opening.

Yet another object of this invention is to provide a lock-pick mechanism to facilitate rapid opening of locks by means of an oscillating implement that imparts a rotary action to the lock cylinder, a spring arm or tension member, and an adapter assembly. The adapter assembly is provided with a clamp and base constructed to be inserted into the keyway of the particular type lock to be opened. The adapter base is designed to provide a space between the base and the lock tumbler pins such that the operator can easily insert a lock pick into the keyway of the lock.

The foregoing objectives and other objectives are accomplished by using an oscillator unit to rotate the cylinder of a lock in a back and forth motion. The motion is transmitted to the cylinder through the adapter assembly base. The adapter base, which comes in different shapes depending upon the particular lock to be opened, is detachably mounted to the adapter clamp. Each adapter base is provided with two openings. One of the openings in the base is to facilitate a fastener screw.

The adapter clamp is provided with a cylindrical stud positioned to fit into the other base opening. This hole and stud alignment resists twisting of the adapter clamp in relation to the adapter base. The adapter clamp is provided with a threaded hole to receive a standard screw or fastener means for holding the adapter base and clamp together in a snug or tight fit. The adapter clamp is provided with four slits or openings arranged to facilitate the insertion of the end of the spring steel arm through one of the slits. The adapter clamp is further provided with two grooves or recesses arranged at a right angle to each other to permit the end of the spring steel arm member to be passed through the slit to seat with one of the recesses such that the edges of the adapter clamp and base will be flush together when joined by the screw-fastener means.

The two grooves are so arranged, and the slits are so positioned such that the tension or spring steel arm member can be turned in various positions at 90-degree intervals throughout 360 degrees. This allows the operator to position the oscillator unit in various positions to obtain the most optimum position to facilitate the opening of a lock. The free end of the tension or spring steel arm member is designed to be inserted into one of two slots or openings carried on the end of the oscillator unit rod. The slots are arranged at a right angle to each other to allow the spring steel arm member to be turned to obtain the most optimum position for the operator. The spring member is secured in the slot with a set screw provided on the end of the oscillating rod.

Once the spring arm is secured between the adapter assembly and the oscillator unit, the lock-opening device is completely assembled and ready for use. In one embodiment, the adapter base of the adapter assembly is inserted in the lower or bottom portion of a lock cylinder plug of a particular lock to be opened. The adapter base selected for this particular lock fits snug in the keyway, thereby avoiding or reducing any lost motion between the spring arm member and the lock cylinder plug. This snug fit permits more efficient application of the oscillation force to the lock cylinder plug and results in less wear-and-tear damage to the adapter base.

It would be impractical to employ an ordinary key as an adaptor base by cutting off its upper portion for at least two reasons. First, their would be so much play between the key base and the lock cylinder plug that a great deal of the oscillation force would be lost. Second, and more importantly, the key base would probably break after a few applications or within a short period of time.

The oscillator unit is pushed in the direction that you wish the lock cylinder to turn. This bends the adapter spring arm member slightly and puts a little pressure on the adapter assembly and the lock cylinder plug. When the lock-opening mechanism is turned on with the switch, the oscillator unit rod moves back and forth, causing the spring steel arm member to move back and forth. This causes the adapter assembly to move the lock cylinder plug back and forth rapidly. Thus, the adapter assembly repeatedly asserts a rotary motion on the lock cylinder plug.

Quick opening of the lock is made possible by inserting a lock pick to the rear of the lock cylinder plug and picking each pin up until all the pins have been picked upward. While holding this vibrating tension on the lock cylinder plug with the lock-opening device, the operator gently turns the lock cylinder plug with the pick in the opposite direction from which the lock-opening device is applying the most of its pressure. The upper pins will then vibrate down to the shear line and the lock-opening mechanism will turn the cylinder open before the tumbler pins can pass the shear line of the lock cylinder.

The lock-opening device oscillates its shaft very fast (approx. 3500 C.P.M.), causing the lock cylinder plug to grip the lock tumbler pins many times and release them many times each minute. The tumbler pins are alternately in a stationary state and a movable state many times a minute. Therefore, they can be manipulated by the operator to open the lock with little difficulty. The lock-opening device will operate when the tumbler pins are raked, picked, or even pushed up all at once. Thus, the operator has a choice of ways to use the device.

The oscillator unit is driven by a small electric motor that has a current rating of less than four amps. This motor can be a standard motor, a two-speed motor, a rechargeable power-pack type motor, or a variable-speed motor. Also, the stroke of the oscillator unit rod can be changed by changing the position of the stud mounted on the driver gear, which carries a bushing that rides in a slot or bracket carried on the oscillator rod. The motor drives a small gear on the end of its shaft. This small gear drives a larger gear called the driver gear. This gives the motor more driving power.

The driver gear has a small stud and bushing on it that fits into a slot on the oscillator shaft. Each time the motor makes a complete revolution, the oscillator rod makes a complete cycle. As the driver gear turns round and round, the oscillator rod goes in and out. As the oscillator rod goes in and out, the spring steel arm or tension member repeatedly asserts the back and forth rotary pressure to the adapter assembly and lock cylinder plug. Also, some of the vibration from the oscillating spring steel arm member is directed to the lock tumbler pins, causing the lock to cleave at the shear line. The tension of the lock-opening device will cause the lock to open.

The lock-opening device of this invention varies from the prior art in several important respects. In the past, instruments were made to strike the lock pins and force them up into the lock case. This damages the pins, making them out of round and scarred. They are left in a condition that is not proper for the best lock operation.

In accordance with this invention, the adapter assembly base does not strike the pins in the lock. The base fits tight in the lock core, and therefore it eliminates any undesired play between the adapter assembly and the lock core. To simply cut the top off of a key and use the bottom portion would not be feasible, since the difference in tolerance would be so great that the key would soon break off. The adapter assembly of this invention fits tight; therefore any play is removed and the adapter assembly is not apt to break off. Also, in the absence of play, the device can impart more back and forth force to the lock cylinder plug The lock opening device moves the lock cylinder plug back and forth very rapidly, causing the lock tumbler pins to be suspended when moved by the lock pick or even by a straightened paper clip.

The lock-opening device of this invention will work with any small piece of strong metal that is of a sufficient size to allow it to move the lock tumbler pins freely. The operator can also use any standard lock pick for this purpose. The top tumbler pins of a lock can be pushed above the shear line of the lock by the operator and then allowed to work themselves down to the shear line when the lock cylinder plug is gently turned back away from the main tension pressure of the lock-opening device. In this way, the tumbler pins are slowed down from movement, yet they are free to move downward as desired by gently removing some of the oscillating tension pressure.

Because of the many tumbler pins in a lock cylinder, with prior lock-opening devices it was very difficult to get all the pins in the proper place because, as they were forced upward, the recoil from the lock springs forced them back downward very rapidly. It took much patience to get them all in the proper position to open the lock. With the lock-opening device of this invention, the pins tend to stay where placed better, and this makes the job of opening a lock easier and faster. In addition, the pins will not be damaged as they might when struck by hard hammer blows from such instruments as lock-pick guns and electric-driven picks.

The lock-opening device of this invention achieves its

objectives by moving the lock plug back and forth very rapidly using a spring steel arm member attached to the adapter assembly on one end and the oscillator unit rod on the other end. As the rod moves in and out, the spring steel arm moves the adapter assembly and the lock plug back and forth. The lock tumbler pins are free to be moved, yet they tend to be held in place long enough for the lock to be opened. In this process, the lock-opening device does not touch the tumbler pins of the lock with any of its parts. The adapter assembly is wedged into the bottom of the lock core and cannot touch the lock tumbler pins. The lock pick is the only instrument that actually comes into contact with the lock tumbler pins. Thus, manipulation of the pins by the operator can be done in a gentle way.

Brief Description of the Drawings

The foregoing objectives and other objects and advantages of this invention will become apparent to those skilled in the art after reading the following description taken in conjunction with the accompanying drawings wherein:

FIG. 1 is a primarily side elevational view of the lock-opening system according to the present invention;

FIG. 1a is a detail sectional view through FIG. 1 on the plane of line 1a—1a;

FIG. 2 is a side elevational view of the adapter assembly portion of the lock-opening system;

FIG. 3 is a side elevational view of the disassembled adapter assembly portion of the lock-opening system;

FIGS. 4 through 8 are side elevation sectional views of the lock-opening mechanism in various stages of opening a lock;

FIG. 9 is a top view of the oscillator portion of the lock-opening system;

FIG. 9a is a detail sectional view through FIG. 9 on the plane of line the 9a—9a;

FIG. 10 is a side elevational view of the oscillator rod

portion of the lock-opening system;

FIG. 10a is a detail sectional view through FIG. 1 on the plane of the line 10a—10a;

FIG. 11 is a side elevational view of the guard assembly portion of the lock-opening system;

FIG. 12 is a front view of a portion of the guard assembly of FIG. 11;

FIG. 13 is a front view of the adapter assembly.

Description of the Preferred Embodiment

The invention herein is described and illustrated in a specific embodiment having specific components listed for carrying out the functions of the apparatus. Nevertheless, the invention need not be thought of as being confined to such a specific showing and should be construed broadly within the scope of the claims. Any and all equivalent structures known to those skilled in the art can be substituted for specific apparatus disclosed as long as the substituted apparatus achieves a similar function. It may be that systems other than lock-opening systems have been or will be invented, wherein the apparatus described and claimed herein can be advantageously employed, and such other uses are intended to be encompassed in this invention as described and claimed herein.

Reference is made to FIGS. 1, 2, and 3 in which various system components are illustrated. The lock-opening mechanism, generally denoted 1, includes the adapter assembly 2, the spring steel arm or tension member 6 and the oscillator unit 7. The adapter assembly is comprised of three major components: the screw-fastener means 5 secures the assembly section together; the adapter clamp 4, which has a tapped or threaded hole 10a to receive the screw-fastener means 5; and the adapter base 3, which is form fitted and interchangeable depending upon the particular keyway of the lock to be opened. The adapter base 3 is designed to provide a different base finger 9 shape for the various types of lock keyways in common use. Each base finger 9 is designed and constructed such that the member does not come into contact with the lock tumbler pins of the lock being opened. The base finger 9 is also designed such that there is sufficient space between the base finger 9 and the lock tumbler pins to permit insertion of a lock pick.

The adapter base 3 is provided with two holes or openings. The hole 10 is arranged to receive the screw-fastener 5 and opening 11 to receive the pin or steel 11a formed on the wall of the adapter clamp 4. The stud 11a extends into the opening 11 in the adapter base 3. The adapter clamp 4 is held very close to the adapter base 3 by screw-fastener 5 to prevent relative twisting motion during use of the lock-opening device. The adapter clamp 4 is provided with four slit openings 13a, 13b, 13c, and 13d for insertion of one end 16 of the arm member 6 through the clamp into one of the grooves 14 or 15. When the end 16 of the arm 6 is placed through one of the slit openings 13 a-d into either groove 14 or 15, the edges of the adapter base 3 and adapter clamp 4 will be flush together when secured together by the screw-fastener 5. The tension arm 6 can be selectively positioned in various directions depending upon which of the slits 13a-d is selected for installation of end 16, and also which of the grooves 14 or 15 is selected. Hence, this allows positioning the oscillator unit 7, carried in casing or housing 8, in a variety of positions to obtain the most optimum position for each application. The opposite end 17 of the tension member 6 is inserted into the opening or slot 34 in the oscillating rod 30, and is held secure by set screw 32. Once the ends 16 and 17 of arm 6 are attached through a slit 13a-d into the adapter assembly and to the oscillator rod 30, the lock-opening system 1 is completely assembled and ready for use.

Referring now to FIGS. 4 through 8, the finger 9 of the adapter assembly 3 is shown inserted into the bottom portion of the lock cylinder 20 and plug 26. When the lock-opening device is turned on, the oscillator unit rod moves the arm member 6 back and forth. This vibration force causes the adapter assembly 3, through base finger 9 to assert a rotary force on the lock cylinder plug 20. As shown in FIG. 5, lock pin 22 is inserted to the rear of the lock plug 26, and all of the lower lock tumbler pins 23 can easily be picked upward. Referring now to FIGS. 6-8, upper tumbler pins 24 will vibrate down to the shear line 25, and the lock-opening device will turn the lock open before the tumbler pins 24 can pass shear line 25, and as shown in FIG. 8.

Referring now to FIGS. 9, 9a, 10, and 10a, the lock-opening device 10 powered by a small electric motor 40, which has a switch 46 and a current rating of less than four amperes. Motor 40 can be a standard motor, a two-speed motor, a variable-speed motor, or even a rechargeable portable power-pack type motor. The motor 40 drives gear 41, which drives a larger driver gear 42. Driver gear 42 has a stud 43 and bearing or bushing 44. The bushing 44 rides in a bracket or slot 45 contained on the oscillator rod 30. The speed of the motor can be varied by changing or adjusting switch 46. Also, the stroke of the oscillator rod 30 can be varied by changing the position of the stud 43, which is mounted on the driver gear 42 and which carries the bushing 44. Each time the motor makes a complete revolution, the oscillator rod 30 also completes a cycle or revolution. As the driver gear 42 turns about its axis, the oscillator rod 30 moves back and forth or inward and outward. Since the rod 30 is attached to the arm member 6, as the rod 30 moves back and forth, the spring steel arm 6 causes rotary and vibrational forces to be applied through the adapter assembly to a lock cylindrical plug 26.

Referring to FIGS. 11 and 12, the lock-opening mechanism includes a safety guard 50. The guard 50 comprises rods 51 and 52 and base plate 53. The guard 50 is mounted on the lock-opening mechanism casing 8 to provide protection for the oscillator rod 30, which is driven back and forth by the driver gear 44.

Other modifications to the above described invention will be apparent to those skilled in the art, and are intended to be incorporated herein.

Having particularly described and ascertained the nature of the lock-opening system, and the manner in which the same is to be performed, what is claimed is:

1. A lock-opening device for unlocking various types of pin cylinder locks comprising:
a. a flexible spring arm member;
b. an adapter assembly having;
    (i) a base member provided with a finger extension having essentially straight, flat top, and bottom surfaces extending substantially parallel to each other,
    (ii) a clamp member;
    (iii) fastener means for detachably mounting one end of said flexible spring arm member between said clamp member and said base member;
c. an oscillator unit having;
    (i) a rotary shaft member for providing a rotary force to said flexible spring arm member, said shaft member provided with detachable fastener means for securing one end of said flexible spring arm member to said shaft member;
    (ii) variable driver means for driving said shaft member at variable speeds and in a back and forth motion to thereby impart a rotary force through said flexible spring arm member to said finger extension and causing rotary forces to be applied to a lock plug, facilitating the opening of the lock without mechanical impact to tumbler pins

2. In a lock-opening device according to claim 1 wherein said finger extension top surface is designed to be spaced out of contact with tumbler pins when inserted into a lock keyway.

3. In a lock-opening device according to claim 2 wherein said clamp member comprises multiple slit openings arranged in grooves to permit installation of one end of said flexible spring arm at the desired angle.

4. In a lock-opening device according to claim 3 wherein said grooves are disposed to form a right angle within said clamp member.